Mar

(Parkers & Rivals)

THE ROLE OF VOLUNTARY ORGANISATIONS

The Role of Voluntary Organisations in Social Welfare

Hugh W. Mellor

CROOM HELM
London • Sydney • Dover, New Hampshire

©1985 Hugh W. Mellor
Croom Helm Ltd, Provident House, Burrell Row,
Beckenham, Kent BR3 1AT
Croom Helm Australia Pty Ltd, Suite 4, 6th Floor,
64-76 Kippax Street, Surry Hills, NSW 2010, Australia

British Library Cataloguing in Publication Data

Mellor, Hugh W.
   The role of voluntary organisations.
   1. Volunteer workers in social service—
   Great Britain
   I. Title
   361.7'0941   HV245

   ISBN 0-7099-3581-1

Croom Helm, 51 Washington Street, Dover,
New Hampshire 03820, USA

Library of Congress Cataloging in Publication Data

Mellor, Hugh W.
   The role of voluntary organisations.

   Includes index.
   1. Charities—Great Britain. 2. Voluntarism—
Great Britain. 3. Associations, Institutions, etc.,
British. I. Title.
HV245.M387   1985   361.7'0941   85-6626
ISBN 0-7099-3581-1

Printed and bound in Great Britain by
Biddles Ltd, Guildford and King's Lynn

CONTENTS

LIST OF TABLES

Tables

NATIONAL VOLUNTARY ORGANISATIONS INTERVIEWED

British Deaf Association   BDA
CHAR (Campaign for the Homeless and Rootless)   CHAR
Chest, Heart and Stroke Association   CHSA
Church Army   CA
Counsel and Care for the Elderly   CCE
Families Need Fathers   FNF
Friends of the Elderly and Gentlefolk's Help   FEGH
Housing Centre Trust   HCT
John Groom's Association for the Disabled   JGAD
Mission of Hope for Children's Aid and
    Adoption   MHCAA
Mutual Households Association   MHA
National Association for the Welfare of
    Children in Hospital   NAWCH
National Gypsy Education Council   NGEC
Royal Association for Disability and
    Rehabilitation   RADAR
Royal British Legion Housing Association   RBLHA
Shaftesbury Homes and 'Arethusa'   Sh. H & A
Stonham Housing Association   SHA
Workers Educational Association   WEA

OTHER ABBREVIATIONS OCCASIONALLY USED

ACC	Association of County Councils
ADC	Association of District Councils
ADSS	Association of Directors of Social Services
AMA	Association of Metropolitan Authorities
DES	Department of Education and Science
DHSS	Department of Health and Social Security
DoE	Department of the Environment
GLC	Greater London Council
HMI	Her Majesty's Inspector (of Education)
LBA	London Boroughs Association
LEA	Local Education Authority
NCVCCO	National Council of Voluntary Child Care Organisations
NCVO	National Council for Voluntary Organisations
NFHA	National Federation of Housing Associations
SSD	Social Services Department

ACKNOWLEDGEMENTS

First I must acknowledge with gratitude the large part played by the chief officers and chairmen of the eighteen sample organisations who gave so generously of their time and thought; and by Raymond Clarke, Secretary of the National Council of Voluntary Child Care Organisations, who became a nineteenth 'witness' as it were: and with them the senior officials of four government departments, the Charity Commission and the Housing Corporation; and officials and members of four political parties. All very busy people, they gave me valuable assistance.

In starting the project, the financial support and general encouragement of the Joseph Rowntree Memorial Trust, and in particular of its Director, Robin Guthrie, was greatly appreciated. In the early stages I had advice in planning the work from Joan Cooper, Geoffrey Beltram and Francis Gladstone: and Joan Cooper, Stephen Hatch and Ian Bruce took enormous pains in reading through my first draft and making valuable comments on it. Professor Robert Pinker did all these things and much else, discussing each chapter with me as it was written, and being my 'mentor' throughout. I am sincerely thankful to them all.

I have received help of all sorts, sometimes essentially anonymous, from numerous others, and I hope that they will treat this vague statement as my acknowledgement to them.

From the first concept of the book to the last page correction my wife Joyce has given me encouragement and help which is uniquely her own, and I could not be more grateful to her.

Finally my thanks go to Barbara Kirkwood and Pamela Pitcher, who have with efficiency and apparent good humour gone through the processes of turning illegible manuscript into camera-ready copy.

Hugh W. Mellor

Chapter 1

INTRODUCTION

[handwritten margin notes: What part do voluntary organisations play in social welfare? Safety net? Choice? Self help? Unpolitical? Essential today? Pressure groups?]

The context of this book is social welfare, and the
assumption is that the state must play a large part
in its provision. What is the future for voluntary
organisations in this context? Before the matter is
examined it is important that the meanings of the
terms 'welfare state' and 'voluntary organisation',
as used by the author, are understood by the reader.
To do this, and to explain the nature of the study
which follows, are the purposes of this chapter.

THE WELFARE STATE

There is no unanimity about the concept of the
welfare state. Many dislike the very name, but it
has come to be widely used. Many books have been
written about its philosophy and its history.
According to the writer's philosophy so will his
history be. Thus Fraser can write: 'In 1536
parishes were authorised to collect money to support
the impotent poor who would thus no longer need to
beg. The state thus acknowledged some minimum
community responsibility for those who were unable
to work' (1). For him the seed was sown in the 16th
Century and grew powerfully in the 19th with the
developments in the Poor Law, Public Health and
Education which took place in the middle years of
that century.
   Another writer dates the birth of the welfare
state precisely as 15th February 1881, when Kaiser
Wilhelm I of Germany proposed to the Reichstag that
social insurance be introduced to protect industrial
workers against the loss of income resulting from
accidents and old age (2). King is not alone in
associating the welfare state with the initiation of
social insurance: it is common to find it said that
the concept was born in Britain with the Liberal

Introduction

government of <u>1906</u>-14, which introduced <u>old-age</u>
<u>pensions, health and unemployment insur</u>ance. 'From
these modest beginnings,' writes Robson:

> the principle emerged that the state should
> eliminate the worst causes of poverty by fixing
> minimum standards of subsistence, medical care,
> education, housing and nutrition by means of
> the social services, minimum wage legislation,
> social insurance and government regulation.
> These <u>minimum standards were</u> established to
> <u>provide a floor below which it was assumed no</u>
> <u>one would be allowed to sink.</u> The minimum
> standards were progressively raised as
> resources increased and confidence grew in the
> new methods.(3)

The man-in-the-street today would I believe not
go so far back. With a little thought he would say
that the welfare state began after the Second World
War: he would associate it with the Beveridge
Report, the National Health Service and a new
education system. As Clegg puts it:

> Starting with the Butler Education Act passed
> by the Coalition Government in 1944, the social
> services took on a completely new look in the
> period up to 1950 and what we call "the welfare
> state" dates from that time although it was
> built on earlier foundations. The overriding
> principle was that <u>services should be</u>
> <u>universal,</u> i.e available to all as of right and
> paid for through the general rates and taxes or
> insurance contributions. <u>The condition of</u>
> <u>receiving</u> help should be need (e.g. of
> <u>secondary education or a doctor</u>) and not
> ability to pay fees. (4)

It is in this sense that I use the term
'welfare state' in this book. I was young in the
1940s. I was inspired by Beveridge's call to tackle
the 'giants' of disease, ignorance, squalor,
idleness and want. I believed then, as I still do,
that <u>government has to play a major part</u> in tackling
them. The essence of the welfare state approach as
I see it is that certain needs will be met,
irrespective of ability to pay, and that a duty is
laid upon the state to guarantee this. With 'the
overriding principle' that services should be
universal, I concur, for without it we shall be in
danger of lapsing again into the 'two nations'

situation of pre-1939, with relatively good
facilities for the well-to-do, and second best for
those who do not have the means to pay for them.
Many of us felt that we had seen the demise of that
situation in the years following the war and do not
want to see it return. As Titmuss wrote in his
'Study about the Role of Altruism in Modern
Society', The Gift Relationship:

> One of the principles of the National Blood
> Transfusion Service and National Health Service
> is to provide services on the basis of common
> human needs; there must be no allocation of
> resources which could create a sense of
> separateness between people. It is the
> explicit or implicit institutionalisation of
> separateness, whether categorised in terms of
> income, class, race, colour or religion, rather
> than the recognition of the similarities
> between people and their needs which causes
> much of the world's suffering.

On the other hand the economics of today may make it
sensible for there to be a limited degree of
'selectivity', whereby people pay something for
certain services if they can afford it, and do not
receive certain public services if they could afford
to buy them elsewhere. To quote Titmuss again:

> The challenge that faces us is not the choice
> between universalist and selective social
> services. The real challenge lies in the
> question: what particular infrastructure of
> universalist services is needed in order to
> provide a framework of values and opportunity
> bases within and around which can be developed
> socially acceptable selective services aiming
> to discriminate positively, with the minimum
> risk of stigma, in favour of those whose needs
> are greatest. (5)

No government, of whatever political
persuasion, appears to have met this challenge: no
positive philosopy is anywhere apparent, and one is
long overdue. Controversy will no doubt continue on
this subject of universalism v selectivity for many
years yet, and it is one of the aims of this book to
take the discussion a little further.
There is another controversy that needs to be
mentioned at this point. It is between those who
have the 'institutional' and those who have the

3

'residual' conceptions of social welfare. The view
of the former is that social welfare is as necessary
to modern industrial society as are roads or a
public water supply. Social and economic
'institutions' such as the national insurance scheme
or National Health Service, designed to provide
social security or care in times of sickness, are
essential. Those who take the other view assume
that the needs of individuals are normally met by
the family and the market economy, but that the
state has a 'residual' function to prevent
destitution and to care for the sick only if, in the
last resort, their families cannot do so; but there
will be strict tests of 'eligibility', and an
implied assumption that it is less worthy to use
public resources than to use private. My approach
to my subject will assume that certain substantial
responsibilities in welfare must remain with the
state, and to that extent, I am of the
'institutional' viewpoint; but that there is much
scope for discussion about what services and
facilities rightly fall within the scope of the
state no one will deny, and this again is a
discussion to which my study may make some
contribution.

My standpoint on the welfare state is therefore
that I assume that the British Government will
continue to accept responsibility for certain major
'welfare' services, the word in this context
including social insurance, a national health
service, public housing, education and employment
services, as well as the personal social services to
which the definition of welfare is sometimes
confined. I assume that in the main these services
will be provided to all who need them, irrespective
of their financial circumstances. I make these
assumptions despite the unhappy restrictions which
the Conservative government which took office in
1979 felt it necessary to make on economic grounds;
and despite certain 'sniping' which has been going
on, not so much against the concept of welfare as
against the place of the state in its provision. As
to the restrictions due to the economic situation, I
am optimistic enough to think that improvements both
in the economy and in our national order of
priorities will rectify them before very long. To
the 'sniping' I must now give a little more
attention.

It comes from three related though different
perspectives. The first arises from a number of
social studies which have shown that care, in its

4

broadest sense, of individuals in need, comes even
today largely from relatives and friends and only to
a modest degree, quantitatively speaking, from the
health and social services. To politicians anxious
to play down the significance of the cuts in public
services, this has been a source of comfort. In the
context of my present exercise it is irrelevant.
The need for public services remains, they came into
existence because informal welfare practices were in
themselves inadequate, and if there are people who
read into current sociological findings that
suddenly the informal is totally capable and the
public services marginal or unnecessary, I am not
one of them.

The second source of 'sniping' comes from the
self-help movement. During the last twenty years
the number of organisations whose memberships offer
mutual aid with particular problems has grown
enormously. They include Alcoholics Anonymous and
the Back Pain Association, the National
Schizophrenia Fellowship and Cruse - the National
Organisation for the Widowed and their Children. As
one directory of such organisations puts it, they
are:

> designed to help people to help themselves by
> providing contact with others who have similar
> problems and by providing access to sources of
> information. People with problems often become
> expert in practical means of coping with them.
> They have the advantage, over professionals, of
> firsthand experience (6).

Some enthusiasts for self-help have gone on to imply
that professional assistance is no longer needed.
For my part, and with the majority of those who have
the utmost respect for these groups, I see them as
partners with, but by no means as replacements for,
the public health and welfare services, and
therefore in no way invalidating my basic
assumptions.

The third of the questioning approaches I have
in mind comes from the practitioners of community
work. They emphasise the importance of the local
context, and aim to mobilise informal and intensely
local effort to deal with social needs. They may
provide information or advice, stimulate self-help
groups, or mobilise resources to press for changed
policies or improved services. For some of these
practitioners, as Professor Pinker relates in his
book The Idea of Welfare,

> this new commitment to localised social action and the nurturing of informal modes of welfare practice is often associated with a hostility towards the administrative ethos of both central and local government,

in contrast to the views of

> the arch-apostles of this administrative tradition ... the Webbs who ... believed that enlightened administrators were the most reliable interpreters of what constituted the best interests of the general public.

Here again, whatever the value of community work, it cannot be seen as a total alternative to central or local government responsibility. The community worker needs specialist back-up, whether for information or advice or for specialist intervention; somebody must appoint (and pay) him/her; and the central or local government department will continue to have responsibility for ensuring a satisfactory level and quality of provision, and for sharing and spreading identified good practice. The welfare state continues to have its place whatever the developments in community work.

It will have been clear from what has already been said that I do not see the welfare state as comprehensive in its provision of services to meet human needs, nor as having a monopoly in the areas in which it does operate. It has an essential and major role in certain fields, but it must always be limited at some point by the resources which it can properly call upon, and at this point in these fields there may still be needs to be met by other agencies. It is inappropriate for the state to undertake some services, and it should never be given a monopoly in any service, lest new initiatives be stultified or the individual be in danger of being sacrificed to the bureaucracy. These considerations bring us to some of the classic arguments for 'pluralism', one of the in-words of the present time. Pluralists maintain that a democratic system requires a multitude of independent voluntary, non-government associations as buffers between the individual and the state. Beveridge himself had a deeply held belief in the importance of voluntary effort, which he thought would, in the society of the future, have a rich variety directed especially at 'the special needs of

untypical distressed minorities'. He saw voluntary
bodies giving 'dynamic individuals with social
conscience' scope for expression of their ideals and
so enabling them to take the place of those with
large personal means and leisure, who were the
pioneers of the past.

Others have pointed out that voluntary
associations have kept the individual from feeling
isolated, protected him from the state, met needs
that could not be filled by the government, and
preserved a degree of choice for him, This brings
me to the second part of my discussion of the
assumptions and definitions that lie behind this
study, to the subject of voluntary bodies.

VOLUNTARY ORGANISATIONS

It is astonishing that as late as 1972 Smith and
Freedman, in their valuable survey of the literature
on voluntary associations, felt it necessary to
state: 'With the exception of a few analysts, most
of the advocates of voluntarism fail even to make
the fundamental distinction between volunteering and
the voluntary association.' (7) In Britain today
such confusion is still to be found, and for this
reason I must make it immediately plain that for my
part I am only incidentally concerned with those
individuals who offer their unpaid services, whether
to statutory or other organisations. I am primarily
concerned with what Blau and Scott call 'formal
organisations', but I must give this concept a more
precise definition. Smith and Freedman defined
their interest as being in:

> structured, formally organised, relatively
> permanent, secondary groupings as opposed to
> less structured, informal, ephemeral, or
> primary groupings, identified, by the presence
> of offices filled through some established
> procedure; periodic, scheduled meetings;
> qualifying criteria for membership; and some
> formalised division and specialisation of
> labour. (8)

Sills writes that definitions of the terms
'voluntary association' differ widely but that they
generally contain three elements:-

> a voluntary association is an organised group
> of persons:

1. that is formed in order to further some common interest of its members;

2. in which membership is voluntary in the sense that it is neither mandatory nor acquired through birth; and

3. that exists independently of the state.(9)

These definitions between them describe very adequately the kind of bodies with which my study is largely concerned, though I shall single out those in the particular field of 'welfare', and particular sectors of that field, as I later explain.

At this point mention should be made of that administrative creature whose existence recently caused much muddying of the water dividing statutory and voluntary organisations – the 'quango'. The self-appointed St George who has been attacking what he sees to be a dragon is Philip Holland MP. In his booklet The Quango Explosion, he writes:

What do we mean by public body? The term is a multifarious one, covering a multitude of different organisations with differing relationships with central or local government. They range from those very similar to Departments of State, quasi-governmental bodies like the University Grants Committee or the Horserace Betting Levy Board, to which problems that central government has taken on have simply been exported, to non-governmental bodies like subsidiaries of the Arts Council. The principal criterion to be applied in determining where along this spectrum a particular body fits is thus its degree of independence. This was the origin of the use of the acronym QUANGO which was invented in the USA during the late 1960s in order to describe the growth of 'not-for-profit' corporations which were nominally non-governmental in character but were, in fact, dependent for contracts on government agencies and were sometimes brought into existence by them: applied thus to many foundations and corporations, QUANGO stood for quasi-autonomous non-governmental organisation. Although in the United Kingdom there have been a few developments of this kind, we use the acronym in its other and more widely understood translation as 'quasi-autonomous national governmental organisation'. A broad definition of the QUANGO to which we refer is 'a body other than a departmental committee to which a Government Minister appoints members other than civil servants.' (10)

It is not surprising that there is confusion in the public discussion of quangos when they are by one person regarded as non-governmental and by the next as national governmental: but the definition Mr Holland finally offers is valuable in that it refers to bodies to which a Minister 'appoints members other than civil servants'. Even if, as perhaps it should, the definition does not say 'all members' it excludes most, perhaps all, of the bodies included in my study, for though many have one or two members (or, more likely, observers) appointed by Ministers, they are usually civil servants. A glance back at the definition of a voluntary association used by Sills will underline the distinction I wish to make: his group 'exists independently of the state', which no quango, however defined, can be said to do. They are not, therefore, included in my study.

Little examination has been made of the history of the development of associations in modern societies (although histories of individual associations have been written), but it seems likely that it was not until the 19th Century that specialised groups began to emerge in Britain. Previously organisations were diffuse, arising substantially from commercial or religious interests, though there were numerous charitable trusts. In medieval times a man might leave land or personal property to the church on the understanding that these gifts would be applied, for example, for the education or relief of the poor, and the ecclestiastical courts would give effect to his wishes. 'In a rudimentary way', writes Chesterman, 'these courts conferred on such bequests privileges similar to those now enjoyed by charitable trusts.' By about 1600 however, the church's role was much reduced. 'On the other hand, a much increased proportion of national wealth was committed through innumerable gifts and endowments (i.e. gifts made on terms that the property given was to be retained as capital and only the income from it was to be spent) to the control of secular trustees and administrators for specific welfare purposes in such areas as education, health and poverty relief.' At this time 'the charitable trust emerged as a major legal mechanism of institutionalised private philanthropy and several key features of the modern law of charities were established.'(11)

The Victorian era saw many charities being established (poverty then being of special concern): a survey in London in 1861 estimated that there were 640 charities there, of which three-quarters had been formed since 1800, and that their income of £2.5 million per annum was greater than the amount spent under the Poor Law in London. Voluntary associations now forgotten started schools and pressed for the universal system of state education of which the 1870 Education Act was the forerunner. The latter half of the 19th Century saw the birth of large numbers of organisations concerned with many aspects of welfare, many of which are still household names today - e.g. Peabody Trust 1862, Dr Barnardo's 1866, British Red Cross Society 1870, National Society for the Prevention of Cruelty to Children 1884.

Since then development has been continuous and steadily more varied, and this applies to both charitable trusts and to voluntary associations. A study undertaken in 1975 showed that about 30% of the charities registered with the Charity Commission had been founded in the period after 1960.(12) Another study in 1977 found that of 635 registered amenity societies, 85% had begun since 1957.(13)

In my definition of voluntary organisations I include charitable trusts as well as associations as defined above. Some associations are registered charities, others are not. Pluralism in social welfare, so far as I am concerned, is not essentially concerned with how the non-statutory sector comes into being, whether it is endowed, or whether it has charitable status at law. I have argued above that though the state has a major role to play, its resources, at least in the foreseeable future, will be limited, and that at this point non-statutory organisations may wish to augment what the state is doing. There will be things the state does not begin to do, again perhaps through shortage of resources, or alternatively because it would not be suitable for it to do so (advising the individual on his relationship with state institutions is an obvious example of this) and voluntary bodies will be left to undertake these kinds of work. Adding particular qualities to what the state is doing is very much the role of the voluntary body: such an organisation can, for example, run an old people's home for residents of a certain religious or philosophical approach to life, so providing them

with companions most congenial to them. The Royal
Commission on the National Health Service recognised
this role of adding particular qualities when in
1979 it reported:

> There is already much public involvement in the
> NHS through organisations such as Hospital
> Friends and the various societies for helping
> particular groups of patient. At one remove
> from the NHS, there are fund-raising and
> research organisations like Age Concern, MIND
> and the Imperial Cancer Research Fund, which
> give valuable help but have a national rather
> than local impact ... We would like to see a
> continuation and expansion of the present
> voluntary effort ...

Because of its independence, and often because
of its relative smallness of scale, the voluntary
body is able to experiment, by doing old things in
new ways, or trying out quite new services, and in
doing so take the risks which might be more
difficult for a large and essentially more
bureaucratic state concern. This independence, as
well as the opportunity to concentrate more single-
mindedly on particular issues or needs, puts the
organisation into a strong position to be a watch-
dog in the field in which it specialises. It also
gives it a chance to develop and promote creative
suggestions for statutory policy. Murray described
this creativity well when he made the sweeping but
encouraging generalisation that in all voluntary
organisations there is a distinct movement from
concentration on the pathology of society to its
positive health, as for example where Marriage
Guidance Councils moved from counselling to
educational work in schools.
   The voluntary body has certain strengths
peculiar to itself. It is by definition, at least
in its early days, motivated by personal
enthusiasms. It counts amongst its supporters those
who are concerned to help individuals with specific
disabilities; or who have a particular cause at
heart, such as certain legislative or administrative
change, and find it more congenial, or consider it
likely to be more effective, to work within a
specialist group rather than a political party; or
who are pleased to give of their specialist
knowledge for a good cause. No doubt there will
also be others, who are in it for the status it
gives; or who count the number of their committee

memberships and have an eye on the Honours List; or
for whom the main attraction is the social life
provided by coffee mornings and other fund-raising
activities; or who hope to see business coming their
way as a result of contacts they make; but even
these supporters are not to be spurned, for they
give in their own way, and can add to the strength
of the organisation if its management is sensible;
and who is to say that those who serve with
apparently loftier motives do not gain as much as or
more than they give?

Apart from their motivation voluntary
organisations have access to certain funds which are
not normally available to the state. In the first
place, those which are charities may be able to draw
on charitable funds established for purposes
compatible with those of the association: and
secondly, they may be able to mount successful
appeals for public subscription, either for a broad
cause or kind of need, or for a specific issue such
as to provide relief after some major disaster.
Statutory bodies have not undertaken this sort of
fund raising though it is true that the Secretary of
State for Social Services has recently considered
allowing NHS establishments to raise charitable
funds: this however seems likely to be restricted
and would raise widespread concern, and difficulty
for the voluntary movements, were it not so.

The Wolfenden Report has shown that today
voluntary social service organisations employ an
appreciable proportion of the paid staff in this
field, and furthermore, that 'taking volunteers and
paid workers together, in the personal social
services the voluntary sector is clearly larger in
terms of manpower than the statutory sector'.(14)
The income of charities of all kinds concerned with
social and environmental services amounted in 1975
to about £1,000 million (15), admittedly only about
3% of what central and local government spent, but
nevertheless appreciable.

For all these reasons I believe that voluntary
bodies and the welfare state have an important
potential future together: but I am aware that the
potential is not always realised, that many of my
statements will be regarded by some as statements of
ideals, not necessarily of realisable facts. When
the Secretary of State for Social Services argued to
the Social Services Committee of the House of
Commons that voluntary community effort may be a
source of imaginative new caring strategies, the
Committee agreed in principle but were 'concerned

[margin note: 1985 figures?]

lest aspiration be mistaken for achievement', and it is precisely this spirit of questioning which motivates my study. It takes me from a description of my assumptions and definitions to a statement of the aims that lie behind this present work.

THE AIMS OF THE STUDY

The main aims of this study are to analyse and comment on the kinds of contributions being made by voluntary organisations in certain sectors of social welfare, and whether and how they relate to the activities of statutory bodies in the same sectors.

If the next thirty years in Britain are to see 'welfare' provided jointly by statutory and voluntary organisations, the bases for their joint action must be adequately accepted by both. In our study we must ask a great many questions. What do the voluntary organisations think the role of the state should be? Do they agree that in certain fields it must predominate and if so how do they see their own roles? If, for example, they provide convalescent homes, or family housing, fields in which the state is very active, have they reasoned out what part they have left to play? Alternatively, if they provide services to which there is no statutory equivalent, is this seen as provisional, until government resources are available for a government service, or is the service seen as essentially one for voluntary control?

Likewise, how do government or local government departments see these matters? By implication, government sees a joint role in certain fields. For example, it disregards certain income provided by Benevolent Funds when assessing an individual's needs for social security payments, so encouraging these Funds to continue: in housing, local authorities and the government-established Housing Corporation have powers or duties to help voluntary housing associations. Do these facts indicate a broadly accepted philosophy about the relative roles of statutory and voluntary, or is this matter subject largely to the whims and fancies of the party political views and expediencies of the day?

Government and voluntary bodies must have respect for and understanding of each other if they are to work together. The presence of criticism one of another does not prove that these qualities do not exist, but some criticisms give one good cause to wonder.

Introduction

The National Federation of Housing Associations, the accepted and highly responsible voice of the movement, not long ago felt it necessary to criticise the government-sponsored Housing Corporation for attempting, through administrative and financial pressures, to re-shape housing associations into a mould of the Housing Corporation's own, 'thereby undermining the diversity of the movement.' That there was at that time a lack of understanding by the statutory body of the essence of voluntary effort few outside the Corporation's own staff doubted.

When in 1980 certain of the government's measures to restrain inflation caused financial support for voluntary organisations to be cut back, a senior civil servant was personally attacked at a meeting with representatives of voluntary bodies for 'obviously not' advising the minister to adopt more congenial policies. That this indicated a woeful understanding of the role of the civil servant, or alternatively a deliberate abuse of the latter's relationship with voluntary organisations, seemed clear. How representative today are these illustrations of lack of understanding?

Respect is another quality, and may or may not accompany understanding. Respect can be built only on a recognition of the efficiency and capability of the other. These in turn rest on a whole range of features, from which a few key issues can be picked out. In this study I shall be concerned only with features of the voluntary movement. To earn respect from government it needs to show that its policies and practices are soundly based. What sources of information does it use? Whom does it consult, and what quality of experience can it draw on within its governing bodies? Is there on the one hand continuity of policy determination, and on the other some element of flexibility? What are the qualifications of its staff? What access has it to the views of the 'consumer' of the social services involved? It must not be possible in the 1980s for someone to write, as occurred in the 1950s, that voluntary societies 'are unscientific in their approach and unbusinesslike in their methods'.(16)

If voluntary organisations are to receive public funds, or indeed if they are to receive substantial support from individual subscribers, it is important that they should give an adequate account of the use made of the funds they receive. Do they produce annual reports and statements of account? Do they provide the information required

14

of them by organisations set up to represent the
public interest, such as the Charity Commission or
the Housing Corporation? Is it as patent as human
affairs can reasonably make it that trust placed in
them is not being abused?

On the other hand, voluntary organisations must
not allow their dependance upon public funds to
cloud their judgement. Madeline Rooff's comments of
twenty-five years ago could be echoed in many places
today:

> It is a considerable temptation to hard-pressed
> voluntary bodies to concentrate upon those
> services which may attract financial support
> rather than upon others which may be of greater
> value but less spectacular in their appeal.(17)

Nor must those who direct public funds expect the
recipients always to toe the official line: it has
been my own experience to hear a warning from a
government department that a voluntary organisation
receiving a grant from that department was not being
wary enough about its pressure group activities.
The balance between accountability and subservience
is a fine one at times. Is it being properly
struck?

Much has been made over many years of the
pioneering role of the voluntary organisation. New
ideas, particularly for practical action, have been
so much regarded as their prerogative by
protagonists of the voluntary movement that it is
hardly surprising that officials of statutory
services have sometimes been resentful. The
implication that local authority social workers, for
example, are bone-headed and powerless to innovate
is manifestly untrue, yet the fact remains that
voluntary bodies have a freedom, within limitations
of their own kind, not available to the public body.
Do they live up to their pretensions in this
respect? Do they produce good ideas and
experimental work?

Of recent years, the type of voluntary body
that has been much in the news has been the kind
that seeks to influence public policy - the 'pure'
pressure group or, more commonly, the organisation
that whilst having practical work for certain kinds
of client to undertake, has a well-developed
'social advocacy' role too. It does not hesitate to
publish its views on a range of issues, to inform
the relevant Minister of State, or to issue press
releases: it may go much further and use more

extensive lobbying and other methods now normal to
the pressure group. It has a freedom to do so,
though limited to a degree if it seeks also to
remain a registered charity. There are a whole
range of other organisations, which, because of
their charitable status or by deliberate choice of
policy, seek to influence social policy in quieter
ways - by discussions in private with those who make
policies, whether they be politicians or civil
servants. Whichever methods are used, again the
proponents of the voluntary movement are apt to make
great play of their influence on affairs; rarely
does any one in the forefront of policy changes
acknowledge their influence, but as no one would
expect them to do so it is easy to explain that
away. But is the voluntary body really having the
effects on policy it sometimes claims? If so, what
of the methods used are the most effective?
        Voluntary bodies should be independent or their
place may be questionable. On the other hand they
will lose respect and effectiveness if they are not
co-operative, one with another, and with the
statutory bodies in the same fields. The
Association of Metropolitan Authorities commented to
the Home Office in 1979 that voluntary organisations
initiate a service, then expect local authorities to
pay for it, and apply their released resources to
other pioneering work, without adequate regard to
'priorities permitted by the limitations of public
expenditure.' New developments, the AMA maintained,
should be 'related to local forward planning
processes' yet 'it is not always easy to secure a
representative view from the voluntary sector'.(18)
A comparison is made between the local authority
world and the world of voluntary organisations; in
the former there are associations (AMA, ADC, ACC)
representing all of their kind in the country in
negotiations with government departments; in the
latter, as Murray wrote in 1969, 'voluntary
organisations do not have one completely accepted
spokesman or even a small group of recognised
spokesmen and so there is not the same ease of
communication as central government has with the
local authority associations.'(19) How far is this
still the case, and how seriously does it affect the
working together whose existence is basic to the
welfare state as my study conceives it?
        This question of course has no validity if
there is no willingness on the part of the state to
work with voluntary bodies whatever their efficiency
and ability to co-operate. Recent research by the

Introduction

National Council for Voluntary Organisations, based
on thirty-two exploratory visits to different areas,
and eight detailed case studies, referred to the
'limited perception of the functions of voluntary
organisations' amongst local authority officers and
councillors and led to the following sombre summary:

> Detailed voluntary involvement in the
> production of new policies and routine
> consultation over the effects of existing
> policies were virtually non-existent. When
> challenged, councillors and officers would put
> up the following obstacles to such involvement:
> lack of voluntary expertise; limited time and
> resources; the responsibility of the local
> authority to mediate between sectional interest
> (which was seen to deny the possibility of a
> particular favoured relationship with the
> voluntary sector); and the requirement of
> democratic accountability (which saw the task
> of representing community interests to the
> authority as exclusive to elected members.(20)

It is not only a question of what attitudes
government and local government departments or
members choose to adopt. There are also built-in
attitudes in the registration, monitoring and
inspection schemes which the state has instituted
for voluntary bodies. All charities must be
registered by the Charity Commission, and must get
its approval for certain kinds of action. Housing
associations which are registered with the Housing
Corporation have access to public funds, but once
registered are subject to considerable scrutiny by
the Corporation. When grants or loans are made by
government or local government conditions will
probably be attached to them.

Then there are initiatives taken towards
voluntary bodies. Government departments will
invite their views, notably these days on Green
Papers. They may positively encourage them to
undertake certain kinds of work, and here the
Voluntary Services Unit of the Home Office is a
notable and recent example (1980) in its offer to
finance 'local voluntary action development
schemes', to stimulate community service, local
charity reviews and neighbourhood trusts. Do such
initiatives have positive and beneficial effects?
And what lies behind them? What do government
departments know about the voluntary bodies to which
they relate? By what standards do they judge them?

Do they accept their basic attitudes? Do they resent them, or positively approve them and accord them the right to take their own decisions, make their own actions, express their own views? We need to know more about the attitudes of government and local government departments to voluntary bodies and my study aims to shed a little light on this matter also.

In the process it may also be possible to judge in a limited way whether pluralism itself is proving, or has the potential, to be the good which my study postulates. It is not without its serious critics. In the USA, according to Smith and Freedman, significant numbers of social scientists have come to see American pluralism as a facade which hides a ruling power elite, and political scientists have questioned the view that non-government groups restrict government power and prevent its abuse. In Britain on the other hand Rose has said that policy makers are a focal point for the ideas and the pressures of organised groups in society, of Parliament, of the party machines, etc. and they respond intuitively to produce the most acceptable decision for the forces they are struggling to keep in equipoise:(21) but President Carter had a comment on this in his farewell address to America in January 1981; he said 'the national interest is not always the sum of all our single or specific interests'. Is there some truth in what Professor Robson, keen supporter of the welfare state and normally moderate commentator on the current scene, has to say? He questions 'whether non-governmental organisations of various kinds in this country exist for the benefit of the nation, or of the state, or of their members, or of themselves and those who manage them', and says that this applies 'even (to) some charitable foundations'. 'Today, pluralism has taken over command of the economy and the social services and threatens the authority of Parliament'.(22)

To answer such a broadside adequately is far beyond the scope of this small book, but I hope to be able to produce some evidence about the qualities prevailing or lacking in the elements of pluralism which I shall be studying, from which the reader can draw some tentative conclusions.

THE FOCUS OF THE STUDY

It will be clear that light can only be shed on this enormous subject by a highly selective focussing.

Introduction

This I do in the first place by concentrating solely
on 'national' organisations. In doing so I do not
forget that services and facilities are directed at
the individual, and in the main this means that
local organisations will be concerned with making
them available: but nearly all local organisations
look for support and guidance from one or more
national bodies, to which they may be affiliated or
of which they are constitutionally a part. National
bodies are therefore of prime importance, and if
their policies are not sound and their practices
efficient it will be very difficult for their local
counterparts to achieve a higher quality.
    This is not to say that I shall be concerned
only with the very large organisations. The Report
of the Goodman Committee on Charity Law and
Voluntary Organisations asked 'What is a National
Charity?' and provided this answer:

> Just as local charities are highly diverse in
> size, purpose and activities, so too are
> national charities. The term 'national' is a
> generic term. It includes charities of all
> sizes but distinguishes itself from 'local'
> charities in that its purposes are nationally
> focussed, either in the sense of having a
> network of branches nation-wide (or at least in
> a majority of counties) or in the sense that
> they focus their attention on some national
> government policy. Even as national
> organisations vary in size so too they are
> constituted according to no set pattern but can
> range from Royal Charter to a simple trust
> instrument.(23)

    Even this description does not do justice to
the diversity of national voluntary organisations,
for although those providing services and facilities
may need 'a network of branches nation-wide', some
will not (e.g. some of those providing information
or accommodation). Those which 'focus their
attention on some national government policy', as
pressure groups or study organisations, are less
likely to have local branches, and if they do such
branches would probably not be 'nation-wide'.
    A focus on national bodies therefore seems
fully justified as a pointer to the state of health
of the genus. No claim will be made that where a
national organisation seems to be first-class all
its subordinate groups will be equally so, but if
some light can be shed on central bodies this should

19

be a valuable step forward to an assessment of the wider situation.

We find ourselves then with an examination of national voluntary bodies in the welfare state. As we have seen, 'welfare' in this context is a wide term. It is historically concerned with the Beveridge giants of Want, Disease, Squalor, Ignorance and Idleness. What I wish to do is to look at those parts of what we may better call the welfare society, in which it is reasonable to assume that voluntary bodies will continue to be substantial partners with the statutory, to see how well that partnership is or could be working.

Not all parts of the welfare society are relevant here. Beveridge himself thought the state alone could tackle the giant Idleness. In his book Full Employment in a Free Society he wrote about a passage in Shirley, by Charlotte Bronte, describing a conversation between a workman and an employer:

> 'Invention may be all right' says the workman, 'but I know it isn't right for poor folks to starve. Them that governs mun find a way to help us ... Ye'll say that's hard to do - so much louder mun we shout, then, for so much slacker will t'parliament men be to set on a tough job.' 'Worry the Parliament-men as much as you please', replies the employer, 'but to worry the mill-owners is absurd.' To look to individual employers for maintenance of demand and full employment is absurd. These things are not within the power of employers. They must therefore be undertaken by the State, under the supervision and pressure of democracy, applied through the Parliament-men.(24)

Whether or not the present British government fully accepts the Beveridge recipe for full employment it seems clear that, like the employers, voluntary organisations, with the exception some might say of the trade unions, cannot provide an answer to the need for employment, although a number of new and old organisations are trying to help the unemployed. They may have a limited role in applying pressure to 'the Parliament men', but a list of organisations in this field does not indicate much activity of this kind, and in any case this seems to be a field suitably omitted from the study.

Beveridge would have liked voluntary bodies to have played a part in tackling Want, voluntary bodies in the rather special shape of Friendly Societies, as he made clear in his book <u>Voluntary Action</u>. This was not accepted by the government of the day, and in any case those Societies could only have been handmaidens of the state. All recent history had shown that the task of tackling Want was too big for voluntary action.

Booth's <u>Life and Labour in London</u> at the end of the 19th Century had made clear how great the unmet need was; it was equally clear that charitable trusts would have to bow out of any prime role in providing income, and central government bowed in, with the Old Age Pensions Act 1908. More recently pensions and national assistance have merged into the broader <u>concept of Social Security</u> which <u>is</u> very much <u>the concern of central government</u>. Nevertheless even today there still remain a substantial number of Benevolent Funds and other charities in the field, offering additional income to specified categories of person at a level now generally very small in relation to income needs, and hardly to be classified within the modern concept of 'income maintenance'. A study of what these bodies achieve, and how they view their future, would have its own values and fascinations, but for my present purposes I have concluded that voluntary bodies can have little future in income maintenance except in the pressure group role. No one can deny the importance, for example, of the Child Poverty Action Group, but this is a specialised field with very few participants in it, and I am omitting it from my study.

So far as the other three giants are concerned, David is still playing a significant part in tackling Goliath. Squalor has been to a degree the target of housing trusts from the earliest almshouses onwards, and the research and propaganda value of voluntary exercises in town planning such as Bournville Village (1895) and Letchworth Garden City (1903) have been enormous. Today we see a <u>surge in the growth of housing</u> associations, most of them taking advantage of the possibilities of obtaining public funds which have grown since those funds were first made available in 1919: today the number of associations registered for this purpose is <u>2,700.</u> As reported recently by the Department of the Environment:

> The number of new dwellings started by housing associations each year increased threefold between 1972 and 1977 and its percentage of the

total public sector output doubled - from 9.5% to 18.4%. Over the same period, its property modernisation work doubled, and its percentage of the public sector output increased from 6.1% to 27.6%. The total dwellings owned by associations now exceeds 250,000.(25)

The movement has of course been set back by current financial restrictions but the potential remains. Most housing associations are not national, but the few that are, and organisations with a focus on national housing policy, are relevant to the study.

In another sector, voluntary organisations' attack on Squalor has been equally impressive, that is the growth in amenity societies. As mentioned earlier, (page 10) a study of 635 registered amenity societies showed that 85% had begun since 1957. They include the Civic Trust (with 1,250 local societies on its register); and Friends of the Earth (with 230 local groups)(26): but these were long preceded by such well-known bodies as the Commons, Open Spaces and Footpaths Preservation Society (1865), and the Town and Country Planning Association (1899). With some reluctance and after much thought I am however excluding these from my study, partly in the knowledge that the number must be kept within bounds, but largely because there is a clear line to be drawn between services for individuals, and services for the public weal. Housing I place on one side, and amenities on the other, of this line.

The government's main attack on the giant Ignorance was launched even before the Second World War ended, in the Butler Education Act 1944. Though there had been state education for three generations previously, only then could it be said to have become universalist. It might have been expected, perhaps hoped, that in the cause of equality the non-statutory sector in the actual provision of 'schooling' would wither away, but it did not. It is not my concern here to discuss the politics of education, for which I am in any case unfitted, but it is necessary to look at the extent of the voluntary sector and its relevance to my study. 'Voluntary' has in my discussion implied 'non-profit' and certainly it is not my intention to examine the functions of private schools, for which profit for the entrepreneurs is certainly the aim. It could be pointed out that the public schools are registered charities, and therefore might fall within my purview. I am however not to be persuaded for that reason to include them: their role is totally different from the general run of organisations with which I am concerned. I must, however, include that modest group of national organisations which are concerned with educational policy, or supplementing the state in ways of their own, for that they have features and functions clearly in common with voluntary bodies in other fields is immediately obvious when one thinks, for example, of the National Adult School Organisation or the National Federation of Voluntary Literacy Schemes.

Finally we come to the giant Disease. This giant has a twin, not clearly identified by Beveridge, called Disablement.* These giants are confronted today not only by medicine but by social work; by the National Health Service, and by the local Personal Social Services. They operate in a field long occupied by charitable trusts and voluntary organisations, whose numbers were expected to decrease after the National Health Service Act 1946, but whose numbers have continued to increase as specialisations of many sorts have become discernible and possible. Services are provided to the home; in clinics and advice centres, day centres

* Footnote

Clegg, in Dictionary of Social Services (27), defines Disablement as:

> A permanent impairment of physical or mental functions e.g. someone with an amputated leg or a condition of mental instability which can be controlled but not cured by treatment. The term as used in the employment and social services usually implies that the sufferer has completed such medical treatment as is likely to improve his condition and, if of working age, needs special help in finding and keeping employment and/or that he needs social (as opposed to medical) help in adjusting to his disability.

There is no doubt that Beveridge would have seen such needs as requiring the intervention of institutionalised services, and probably included them under 'Disease' though incorrectly so according to modern concepts and indeed according to the Oxford Dictionary.

and day hospitals. There are out-patients and in-
patients, in hospitals and in other accomodation,
for particular types of need. In this field, as in
education, the private sector also has a major place
which will not be covered by our study but which
must not be overlooked. In sheer numbers however,
voluntary bodies in this sector of the study are
greater than in any other.
     So we find ourselves with a brief which is
reasonably clear, in theory at least: a brief to
look at national voluntary organisations specifically concerned with certain client needs, and
operating in the fields of housing; of education
with certain qualifications; and of the health and
personal social services. Our brief is in
particular to study what links there are between
national voluntary bodies and the state, and to
consider how far they are affected by inadequate
understanding on the part of either, or inadequate
qualities or capacities on the part of the
voluntary.
     No recent study that I have been able to
discover has done more than touch upon this aspect,
or looked very closely at how voluntary
organisations go about their work. Certain recent
works might reasonably have been expected to do one
or both of these things, the most notable of which
is the Wolfenden Report, which spoke of how 'the
volume and vigour of voluntary activity make it a
sufficiently important element in our national life
to deserve a dis-passionate and considered
appraisal.' The report analysed helpfully the role
of voluntary organisations in relation to the
statutory system: had a chapter on Central
Government and the Voluntary Sector, which concluded
that 'the pluralist philosophy is generally accepted
by both political parties', and discussed somewhat
academically the extent to which government grants
rightly involve government influence. It described,
at considerable length and with evident approval,
the traditional roles of 'intermediary bodies', both
specialist and generalist (e.g. National Council for
Voluntary Organisations as it now is). However, it
was only in passing that it dealt with 'on the job'
relationships between voluntary bodies and
government departments; it looked in only very
limited ways at how the former organise themselves
and go about their work; and at times it left the
reader confused as to where it was discussing local,
and where national, bodies - let alone what sort of
body.

24

Introduction

The government, in the form of the Voluntary
Services Unit of the Home Office, followed up the
Wolfenden Report by issuing its own discussion
document (28), and later a report on the comments
that document elicited. The role of the national
voluntary body had strikingly little attention in
both these documents.
A study undertaken by the ill-fated Personal
Social Services Council in 1975 commented on the
'stark fact ... that no one in either the statutory
or voluntary sectors possesses much detailed
information on the size, scope, nature and
development of voluntary organisations' activities.'
'There remains a source of uncertainty about the
relationship between statutory and voluntary
organisations' and a lack of 'a theory which would
specify the role of voluntary organisations in a
complex industrialised society which boasts a
substantial system of state social services.'(29)
The Wolfenden Report itself noted that 'despite
growing interest in the voluntary sector, the
absence of systematic studies during the past twenty
years is notable'. One that there was requires
special mention - Voluntary Organisations and Social
Welfare by G.J. Murray.(30) The subtitle An
Administrator's Impressions indicates clearly what
the book is, and where its value lies: in a year's
sabbatical leave a senior government official gave
himself the following aims:

1   to look at (voluntary organisations)
     individually for their own organisational
     characteristics;
2   to look at their relations with each
     other;
3   to consider the impact of local and
     central government upon them.

There was real value in having a government
official's comments on voluntary organisations,
particularly so as Murray starts with understanding
and apparent sympathy without letting these cloud
his objectivity.
The excellent short book which resulted has
been a real source of inspiration to me, and if my
own contribution can be said to build upon, extend
and up-date Murray's work of 13 years previously I
shall be gratified. My regrets are that it seems
not to have had the attention it deserved, and that
it has been out of print for some years.
One other important work must be mentioned at

this point, Voluntary Agencies in the Welfare State
by Ralph M. Kramer. A cross-national study of
voluntary agencies helping disabled people,
published in 1981, it covers some of the aspects
with which I am concerned, and I quote and compare
its findings as appropriate in later chapters.
  In the next chapter I move on from this
discussion of the broad approach I have set myself
to a more detailed description of the practical
implications, and the methods used in carrying out
the investigation.

REFERENCES

1. Fraser D. The Evolution of the British Welfare
     State. MacMillan, London, 1973.
2. King, Anthony. "Bismark was right about the
     welfare state". Article in The Times,
     23rd February, 1981.
3. Robson, W.A. Welfare State and Welfare Society.
     Illusion and Reality. George Allen and
     Unwin, London, 1976.
4. Clegg, Joan. Dictionary of Social Services.
     Bedford Square Press, London, 1977.
5. Titmuss, R.M. Commitment to Welfare. George
     Allen and Unwin, London, 1968.
6. Sunday Times Self-Help Directory. Ed. Judith
     Chisholm and Oliver Gillie. Times
     Newspapers Ltd, London, 1975.
7. Smith, C. and Freedman, A. Voluntary Associa-
     tions. Perspectives on the Literature.
     Harvard University Press, Cambridge,
     Massachusetts, 1972.
8. Ibid.
9. Sills, D.L. "Voluntary Associations:
     Sociological Aspects", in International
     Encyclopedia of the Social Sciences, Vol
     16, 363 - 367. Collier-MacMillan, 1968.
10. Holland, P. and Fallon, M. The Quango
     Explosion, (p.7). Conservative Political
     Centre, London, 1978.
11. Chesterman, M. Charities, Trusts and Social
     Welfare. Weidenfeld and Nicolson, London,
     1979.
12. Austin, M. and Posnett, J. "Charitable
     Activity in England and Wales", in Social
     Policy and Administration, Vol. 13, No. 3,
     Autumn 1979.

13. Barker, A. and Keating, M. "Public Spirits: Amenity Societies and Others", in Crouch, C. British Political Sociology Yearbook, Vol. 3, Participation in Politics. Croom Helm, 1977.
14. See The Future of Voluntary Organisations, Report of the Wolfenden Committee, (p.36). Croom Helm, London, 1978.
15. Ibid. (p.252).
16. Rooff, Madeline. Voluntary Societies and Social Policy. Routledge and Kegan Paul, London, 1957.
17. Ibid.
18. Association of Metropolitan Authorities. The Government and the Voluntary Sector, Comments on the Home Office Document. (Unpublished) 1979.
19. Murray, G.J. Voluntary Organisations and Social Welfare. Oliver and Boyd, Edinburgh, 1969.
20. Unell, Judith; Leat, Diana; and Smolka, Gerry. "Planning Local Service. Rhetoric and Reality", in Voluntary Action, Winter, 1980.
21. Rose, R. (Ed.) Policy-making in Britain. A reader in government. MacMillan, London, 1969.
22. Robson, W.A. Welfare State and Welfare Society. Illusion and Reality. George Allen and Unwin, London, 1976.
23. Charity law and Voluntary Organisations. Report of the Goodman Committee. National Council of Social Service, 1976.
24. Beveridge, William H. Full Employment in a Free Society, (p.16). George Allen and Unwin, London, 1944.
25. Department of the Environment. Housing Associations and their part in current housing strategies. 1979.
26. Op.cit.
27. Op.cit.
28. The Voluntary Services Unit, Home Office. The Government and the Voluntary Sector. 1981.
29. Personal Social Services Council. Adrian Webb, Lesley Day, Douglas Weller. Voluntary Social Service Manpower Resources. 1976.
30. Op.cit.

Chapter 2

SAMPLING AND FIRST IMPRESSIONS

employment
disease — disabled
education
housing

ORGANISATIONS TO BE SAMPLED

In the first chapter we discussed the broad aims of
the study. We were reminded of Beveridge's
'giants', for whose demise the welfare state was
founded. It was postulated that certain of the
giants would need to be tackled jointly by statutory
and voluntary organisations, and we fastened
particularly on Squalor, Ignorance and Disease, with
the latter of which was coupled the twin,
Disablement. The aim is to know how well equipped
the voluntary organisations are to play their part
in this battle, and whether strategy and tactics are
well co-ordinated by them and their more powerful
comrades-in-arms, the various authorities through
which the state plays its part.
     Our first step towards this goal must be to
establish a comprehensive list of the organisations
in which we are interested. We were fortunate in
having a basic document prepared and published by
the National Council for Voluntary Organisations,
entitled Voluntary Organisations. An NCVO Directory
1980/81. It lists the names of over 500 national
voluntary bodies, together with summaries of their
aims and activities. 'Voluntary organisation' is
interpreted, the Directory says, 'as a self-
governing body of people who have joined together
voluntarily to take action for the betterment of the
community'. Its scope is however much wider than
ours, being concerned for example with animal
welfare and the arts, human rights and international
action, as well as with housing and health,
education and handicap. From it however, we can
fairly readily draw a list of bodies in the fields
with which we are concerned, and without it that
task would have been immensely more tedious and

28

undoubtedly less comprehensive.

The other directory with obvious relevance is
Charities Digest, published by the Family Welfare
Association, of which the 1981 edition was available. It states that its aim is 'to concentrate on
charities which provide a service to the individual'. Though it states that it is 'not confined to
charities registered under the Charities Act 1960,
but includes also some charities which are exempt
from registration and a number of local authorities
and non-charitable bodies whose addresses are
thought likely to be useful', its scope is clearly
more limited in relation to the present study than
that of the NVCO. It is not, for example, basically
concerned with pressure groups, whereas these are
encompassed by the NCVO Directory. Nevertheless,
Charities Digest shows that the NCVO Directory is
not all-inclusive, for it provided some additional
names which it seemed appropriate to include on our
list: moreover there were five others in relevant
fields which came to the writer's notice, which were
in neither publication, and which have been included
on his final list.

This latter fact points to the need at this
stage to enter the caveat that the list finally
prepared cannot be totally comprehensive. If NCVO
and the Family Welfare Association, bodies which are
long established and with extensive contacts, miss
some references, who else could claim to be more
successful? It has also to be accepted that what to
include on the list is a matter of judgment. All
the time probably new organisations are being
formed. Some of them will prove to be shallow and
short-lived, and ought not to be included in any
study of long-term issues. Certainly no one with
any sense of responsibility should take a voluntary
organisation at its face value, or even rely too
much on its letter-heading. It is the value of
using directories published by reputable and long-
established organisations that superficial and
ephemeral bodies are unlikely to be included. On
the other hand it does seem that certain bodies may
be rejected for inclusion by such publishers which
should have been accorded greater respect. In
general however, it can be confidently claimed that
the organisations which were the subject of this
study formed the bulk of those in existence which
have serious and relevant aims, and that conclusions
drawn from them are representative of the whole.

The use of these directories eliminated,
because of their date of preparation, any

organisations which came into existence in 1980 or
later. This meant that by the time any approach was
made to them they would have been in existence for a
minimum of hardly less than two years. This
provided a cut-off point which would have had to be
imposed had it not been automatic, for many of the
questions we wished to discuss could not have been
adequately answered, or answered at all, by those
with only a few months' existence and no time to
have set up their organisations and established
their methods of working.

The NCVO Directory provided a further automatic
sorting, for the Council covers England only, having
autonomous counterparts in Wales, Scotland and
Northern Ireland. This sorting was welcome, for it
would not have been possible within the limitations
of the writer's time to look further afield. The
Directory does however include a number of
organisations whose main emphasis is on overseas
work, such as the Commonwealth Society for the Deaf
and the Ockenden Venture, and names of organisations
of this sort were struck off the list at the
beginning.

In preparing the final list of bodies for this
study it proved necessary to refine the definitions
on which we settled in Chapter 1, even further.
First it was clear that some of the bodies referred
to in the directories did not fall into our
definition of 'national', which was that of the
Goodman committee - 'having a network of branches
nation-wide (or at least in a majority of counties)
or in the sense that they focus their attention on
some national government policy'. Though even this
definition is not crystal clear, it was evident that
certain organisations did not fall within it and
they were excluded.

A further group of bodies was left out because
they were purely 'back-up' organisations, whereas
our study is concerned with bodies 'specifically
concerned with certain client needs'. Thus we did
not include Action Resource Centre which arranges
the secondment of people from business and industry
to community projects or ARVAC (Association of
Researchers into Voluntary Action and Community
Involvement): or funding organisations such as
Sainsbury Family Charitable Trusts or Help the Aged.
Nor did we include what the Wolfenden Report called
generalist intermediary bodies, in particular the
National Council for Voluntary Organisations, the
Volunteer Centre and Community Service Volunteers.
We excluded very specialised organisations, largely

used by, or dependent on referrals from, other bodies: amongst them were, for example, the Albany Trust (sexual identity and relationship problems), the Foundation for the Study of Infant Deaths, and the British Library of Tape Recordings for Hospital Patients.

On the other hand the list did include a number of specialist intermediary bodies, in the Wolfenden definition, for most if not all of them have very direct relevance to 'certain client needs' e.g. National Association of Citizens Advice Bureaux or the National Marriage Guidance Council, and may have service or social advocacy functions in addition.

When we began to examine more closely the nature of those remaining, all now within specific fields of interest, we found further refinement necessary within the health sector. First, we had to subtract bodies concerned with public health, as opposed to health services: the National Society for Clean Air, for example, excellent though its aims are, is not directly concerned with client needs. Secondly, there were a considerable number of bodies concerned with clinical matters, such as the National Ankylosing Spondylitis Society, or oriented very closely to a specific disease or condition, even though providing certain non-clinical services, such as the British Migraine Association or the Mastectomy Association of Great Britain. Such bodies, it seemed, would relate mainly to the medical profession rather than to statutory services in the sense we have had in mind; they are also somewhat on a par with the very specialised bodies already rejected, and therefore - with some reluctance, for their importance is obvious and it would have been interesting to include them - it was decided to omit most of them from the list, unless they had a wider personal service coverage as well as a specialised clinical emphasis.

Finally, within the health and social service sector, there is a large group of organisations, most of which have been formed within the last twenty years, many within the last ten, which may be described as 'self-help' or 'mutual aid'. These were briefly referred to in Chapter 1. Beveridge made the distinction between mutual aid and philanthropy, though seeing the former at that time largely in terms of financial support, epitomised by the Friendly Societies. Blau and Scott, classifying organisations into four types according to beneficiary, distinguish between 'mutual-benefit'

associations, whose beneficiaries are the
membership, and 'service organisations', whose
beneficiaries are the clients. Only recently,
because of the comparative newness of the self-help
movements in our present field of concern, have
systematic analyses been made of its participants:
one of these was published in 1977 - Robinson and
Henry: Self-Help and Health. Mutual Aid for Modern
Problems. It makes clear that these associations
are based on the common experience of members, and
are run by these members and for these members. The
process of self-help in most of them is dependent on
joining a group of people with similar problems.

> Self-help works for people with persistent
> problems ... by transcending the short-term
> solutions of conventional problem-solving. In
> self-help the problem is integrated with life.

Yet most of them do not look beyond the immediate
concerns of their members, and could not be regarded
as likely partners of the state, the relationship
with which is the major interest of this study. For
these reasons, again after some travail of mind, it
seemed that most of these associations should be
excluded from the list, though one or two which the
reader may regard as mutual-aid will be found there,
generally on grounds that there is evidence of a
wider participation, a wider perspective than that
of a membership of people with common disabilities.
The judgment has had to be that of the writer, based
on the NCVO Directory, and - like all the decisions
referred to in this chapter - will no doubt be
subject to some criticism from some quarters.
    The decision should not be interpreted as a
comment on the significance of mutual aid
organisations. Their value must be considerable at
any time, and particularly so at a time when
resources for client-oriented services are severely
restricted. A valuable contribution to discussion
of their role was published by ARVAC in 1980,
entitled Mutual Aid and Social and Health Care, Ed.
Stephen Hatch; and a Directory of National
Organisations concerned with various diseases and
handicaps was published in the same year as Self-
Help and the Patient by the Patients' Association:
it is of interest that only a small proportion of
the organisations appearing in the latter are to be
found also in the NCVO Directory. In 1983 another
useful survey was published: Self-Help and Social
Care: Mutual Aid Organisations in Practice, by Ann

Sampling and First Impressions

Richardson and Meg Goodman.

METHOD OF SAMPLING

These various eliminations resulted in a list of 150
organisations, whose names may be seen in Appendix
A, with their dates of formation where known.
Having prepared our list the question was how best
to use it in the service of our investigation. In
one way or another it had to be used to provide a
sample for closer study. There were various
possibilities. It could be stratified by sector of
the field - housing, education, health services,
social services. It could be stratified by client
need - for advice, accommodation, treatment,
physical care or education. Or by kind of client -
child, parent, old person, handicapped person. Or
by the function of the organisation - to educate,
exert political pressure, provide a domiciliary
service or residential care. Or by the age of the
organisation, so as to get a balance between those
long established and those quite new. All of these
possibilities have their attractions, but all were
ultimately rejected, for two reasons, one
fundamental and one technical.
   To take the technical reason first, it was
clear that the number of organisations it was going
to be possible to study would not be large enough to
enable us with confidence to say that our sample was
representative of more than certain very broad
groupings. This however, was a much less important
reason than the fundamental one that to undertake
such a stratification at all probably misconstrues
the real aim of the study, which is to draw broad
conclusions which may be of value right across the
whole field. The aim is not to attempt to assess
the professional or specialist contribution which
any organisation makes in its particular field, e.g.
on foster care, marriage guidance or residential
care of the elderly: but rather to consider matters
common to them all, - how they are organised,
whether they get a steady supply of enthusiastic
support, what quality of information and advice they
can depend on, whether they are able as required to
develop creative ideas and practices, what they see
to be their responsibilities to consumer or
supporter: and how all that they do relates to
their statutory counterparts, in theory and in
practice, - what mutual understanding and respect,
and what machinery for collaboration, there is. In
the tapestry which depicts the voluntary

contribution to the welfare society these are as it were the warp, whereas the specific roles of each organisation are the weft.

We are interested in voluntary organisations as such, what they are doing and are capable of doing, what they have to teach one another and those in statutory bodies, and our list of 150 bodies is in this respect rightly regarded as homogeneous, and to sample from it in a stratified way is unnecessary. For these reasons it was decided that a straight sample of one in ten would provide valuable and representative information. Random numbers were used to take the sample.

INFORMATION TO BE OBTAINED

It is easy enough to write down all that one would like to know about the voluntary movement. It would be possible, though much less easy, to construct ways of answering the questions one had raised, if one had a substantial team of variously qualified researchers and plenty of time available for them to go about the task. It is perhaps even less easy to construct a manageable though productive programme for a one-man exercise, though the very limitation of manpower settles a number of issues. It was clearly impossible to carry out extensive in-house examinations of files and other records of the organisations selected - though certain straight facts can readily be obtained and do speak for themselves. It is clear that much must depend - as in any social research of this kind of whatever size - upon the co-operation of those who run the organisations involved, but that in this case it must depend particularly upon what may be learnt from only one or two individuals.

In this study middle management had to be excluded as a major source of information, nor could information be sought from clients: the study had to depend upon the top level of the structure, but this is justifiable not only on grounds of lack of resources, but also because this is not a study of administration or management. It aims largely to describe factors of interest to informed members of the public, of other voluntary bodies, and of departments of state, who are interested in the quality of the output of voluntary bodies.

The exercise was planned therefore on the basis of interviews, first with the chief executives (often known now as Directors, earlier as Secretaries) of the voluntary bodies listed in the sample; and secondly the chairmen and at their discretion possibly other members of executive committees. From the chief executive it would be possible to obtain basic facts about the organisation. What client needs are its concern? What major ways of meeting them come within its remit? Does it publish an Annual Report? What is its committee structure? How are members elected or selected? What are the main sources of funds? In what ways is their use restricted? What is the geographical coverage of the work the organisation does? What other organisations, voluntary and statutory, are in the same field? What contacts are maintained with them? What sources of information are available to the organisation? What staff are there and what are their qualifications? And so on.

From the chairman a different perspective would be anticipated, more substantially on wider policy, though it seemed likely that the balance of knowledge and vision, immersion in policy or in detailed administration, which would be found between chief executive and chairman would vary greatly. Though the meeting with the chairman could have a different agenda, there would be considerable overlap with what had been discussed with the chief executive: the latter would almost certainly be present with his chairman, and many of the questions would be answered jointly. Nevertheless it was important to have separate access to the views both of staff and committee, particularly where matters of judgment were concerned: and discussion of the main aims of the organisation, of how ideas and policies are developed, of accountability to those who support the work in any way, of relationships with government, to take but a few examples, are matters with which, it was assumed, committee members would be especially concerned. It was planned to have long interviews, on a semi-structured basis, in each case. Supplementary information would be sought later.

The study would then still be far from complete; an attempt was to be made to see the work of each organisation from the other side of the voluntary-statutory divide, to find out how government viewed what the organisation was doing: and this implied a further series of interviews, of three kinds. The first was with the government departments mostly concerned with each voluntary organisation: if in health or social services, the Department of Health and Social Security; if in education, the Department of Education and Science;

if in housing, the Department of the Environment, and so on. Did the department see the organisation's work as supplementary to statutory services? If so, were the two well co-ordinated, and how? Or was the organisation's work of a nature different to any statutory service? What was the department's view of its value? What influence did the voluntary body have on statutory provision, whether by example, or by pressure-group activity? Did the department find the voluntary organisation useful as a source of information or ideas for itself? What in general was the voluntary body's role in policy making, if any?

Policy making is traditionally a party matter, though there are some who would say that the initiative on certain issues has passed to specialised pressure groups. Whether there are links between party and pressure group is in any case of importance, and the second series of interviews was therefore with political parties, to discuss with them the extent to which they used specialised voluntary bodies in the 'welfare' field, for information, ideas, policies. Did they maintain regular links in any way, e.g. by using certain people as advisers, by having joint meetings or working parties? Did they refer enquirers to specialist voluntary bodies? 'The professional politician', wrote Rose, '... can only find an opportunity to discipline himself to long-term thinking when he is in opposition.' Does the professional politician in opposition use the voluntary organisation for this purpose? These questions and others, related particularly to the voluntary organisations in the sample, were the subject of interviews with the Conservative, Labour, Liberal and Social Democratic parties.

Finally, there were to be interviews with a number of government agencies having particular responsibility for voluntary bodies. Organisations with charitable status must register with the Charity Commission, which has certain responsibilities for supervision of their affairs. Housing associations which wish to make claim on public funds must now register with the Housing Corporation, whose monitoring and other powers over what they do is now considerable. The Voluntary Services Unit of the Home Office was established to promote a co-ordinated approach to voluntary bodies among government departments, and to seek 'to develop fruitful contacts between voluntary organisations and central government.' Local

government too has extensive contacts with voluntary
bodies, mainly perhaps at local level, but also with
national voluntary organisations through the three
local government associations, the Association of
County Councils, the Association of Metropolitan
Authorities, and the Association of District
Councils. It was clearly important to know how all
these departments and associations viewed the
present and future work of the bodies under review,
and to understand their relationships with them, and
interviews were sought to this end.

THE SAMPLE

A random sample of one in ten of the organisations
was taken. To it was added two national housing
organisations, Royal British Legion H.A. and Stonham
H.A., for though housing associations are a very
particular type of voluntary organisation, because
of the extent of their dependence on statutory
funding, the relevance of their expertise to many
aspects of our study is considerable. The two
organisations used as pilots were also included
(Counsel and Care for the Elderly, and Housing
Centre Trust), though their evidence will be
identified as such where this would in any way alter
the emphasis or conclusions.
    One organisation in the initial sample,
Campaign for the Advancement of State Education, had
to be omitted from the list, as it made no response
to approaches, was found to have left the address
and telephone number listed in the directory and was
not listed elsewhere.
    The organisations finally listed for study
therefore number eighteen and will be referred to as
'the sample' in future. The list is set out for
ease of reference at the beginning of the book, and
their objects as officially stated are set out in
Appendix B. All of them are charities.
    A more precise analysis of how the sample
compares, in the kinds of activity it represents,
with the total population of organisations, can be
obtained by relating it by category to those in
each category in the NCVO Directory. The results
are set out in Table 2.1.
    The list includes long established and quite
new organisations, with a spread of age not
dissimilar from the total population as Table 2.2
shows.

Table 2.1: The Sample by Category of Activity

Category of Activity	No of Orgs in Total Population (Directory)	No of Orgs in Sample	Col (3) as % of Col (2)
(1)	(2)	(3)	(4)
Child Care	25	3	12.0
Education	8	2	25.0
Elderly	10	2	20.0
Family and Parental Welfare	17	4	23.5
Health and Handicap	28	5	17.9
Housing	33	7	21.2
Offenders	7	2	28.6

It should be borne in mind that some organisations are classified in more than one activity category.

Table 2.2: The Sample by Date of Establishment

Date of Establishment	Organisations in the sample		Orgs in Total Population	
	No of Orgs	% of Orgs	No of Orgs	% of Orgs
Before 1900	5	27.8	33	22.0
1900 - 1919	2	11.1	10	6.7
1920 - 1945	2	11.1	21	14.0
1946 - 1969	4	22.2	59	39.3
1970 - 1979	5	27.8	26	17.3
Not known	-	-	1	0.7
Totals	18	100.0	150	100.0

It is evident too that the scale of operation of the bodies in the sample varies enormously. A rough guide to this may be obtained from the figures of annual income from all sources (including legacies), obtainable from the latest statements of accounts that were available. The figures relate only to income of the national body, and not to branches or affiliated organisations: but our study is of national bodies so the figures have real significance. They are set out in Table 2.3.

Table 2.3: The Sample by Annual Income *

Organisation	Annual Income (all sources)
	£
BDA	346,000
CHAR	76,000
CHSA	886,000
CA	3 - 4,000,000
CCE	204,000
FNF	1,500
FEGH	1,943,000
HCT	52,000
JGAD	1,012,000
MHCAA	217,000
MHA	1,140,000
NAWCH	72,000
NGEC	1,000
RADAR	690,000
RBLHA	6,000,000
Sh H & A	455,000
SHA	900,000
WEA	91,000

The organisations in the sample vary in other ways. Although RADAR is the only one that is a fully-fledged 'intermediary' organisation in the Wolfenden definition, there are at least two others, BDA and WEA, whose roles may be said to approximate to it, in that they have large numbers of branches looking to them.

* Footnote

In 1983 the Charities Aid Foundation published Charity Statistics 1982/3. In it there is a table, in order of size of total voluntary income, of the top two hundred grant seeking charities in all fields. Thirty-eight of the 150 in our population appear there, and four appear in our sample. They are however 26th, 29th, 30th and 33rd out of 38, so none of the very wealthiest are covered by our study.

Five of the organisations may be said to have pressure group roles - CHAR, FNF, HCT, NAWCH and NGEC - varying from the single-issue approach in FNF and NGEC, through the multi-issue CHAR and NAWCH, to the very eclectic approach of HCT. Two organisations are totally member-orientated, with no paid staff, and one has only recently appointed a paid chief officer: the others are fully-developed, in the sense of having a clear member-staff division of roles.

As might be expected, several of the organisations have specific or near-specific religious origins, aims or regulations. The MHCAA insists on evangelical control of its activities; the Church Army defines its first aim as evangelism and makes membership of the Church of England a condition of its own membership; Shaftesbury Homes and 'Arethusa', and John Groom's Association for the Disabled are both very conscious of their religious objectives, and refer to them in their Memorandum and Articles of Association.

Otherwise the sample organisations are involved in a variety of activity, mostly providing some service or facility, one or two developing pressure group interests as well. With the benefit of hindsight one might have hesitated about including certain of them in a study of national bodies: MHCAA, for example, is restricted in its provision of residential care to the area in which its offices are situated, though its adoption service is nation-wide. This, however, became known only as the study progressed, and conclusions that it draws refer to, and allow for, such qualifying factors as the two or three organisations concerned may impose. There is every reason to believe that the sample is so varied that it brings to light a great many of the issues which need discussing at the present time.

FIRST IMPRESSIONS

Approaches were made to all the organisations by a standard letter, a copy of which comprises Appendix C. It asked for co-operation in providing information, initially by post, but then by interviews with the Chief Executive Officer (variously described in the organisations concerned as Director General, Director, General Secretary, Chief Secretary or Secretary), and (on a separate occasion) the Chairman with or without the CEO. In most cases there was no difficulty in arranging to

see the CEO and the interview took place within two
months of the first approach. In some cases the
first response was cautious - researchers are,
perhaps with some justification, looked upon with
suspicion or alarm in certain quarters: this was
epitomised by the person, who, at the second
reminder by telephone after two months delay,
exclaimed "Oh God, you're the one who wants a lot of
information and I've been putting it off." In two
cases caution appeared to extend to real resistance,
but when this was overcome co-operation was warmly
extended, and ultimately this could be said of every
one of the CEOs.

On three occasions arrangements were delayed by
letters going astray, but it is probably significant
that the greatest communication problems arose with
one of the two organisations (FNF) which did not
have an office or permanent organisation address.
The first problem was that there had been a change
of honorary secretary since the directory appeared.
A phone call to NCVO provided the address of the
new secretary, but no reply was received to a letter
to that address. There was no telephone number in
the Telephone Directory, but one was obtained from
the National Children's Bureau. That number was
unobtainable, and Directory Enquiry pronounced it
'temporarily out of service' at the request of the
Telephone Manager. Only after further research
identified the name and telephone number of a member
of the committee could normal arrangements be made.
My approach was perhaps by chance at an unfortunate
moment in the organisation's affairs, and there is
no intention here of singling out this one body for
criticism: processes might well have been smooth
and easy on another occasion, as they were in the
case of my approach to the other organisation (NGEC)
which had no office address; and it must be added
that when I saw him the chairman of FNF made a point
of saying that he wanted to open an office in
London. It is clear that without at least a
permanent address quite small things can provide
hazards for people who wish to make contact unless
they are very determined and 'know the ropes': as a
result a client may not be helped, or a useful
contact not be made.

The next stage, of seeing the chairmen, was in
three cases effected as it were without request. On
my visit to the director of NAWCH I found the
chairman there too, and - as the latter's baby-
sitter was unavailable - the chairman's two-year-old
baby with her, which made for a somewhat less formal

interview than it would otherwise have been. The
contact ultimately made with FNF was immediately
directed to the chairman, who 'stood-in' for both
interviews at once: and the person approached as
honorary secretary of NGEC turned out to have become
the current vice-chairman, who brought in the then
honorary secretary and again provided a composite
interview for both levels.

In all, thirteen chairmen, two vice-chairmen
and one honorary treasurer (the chairman being ill
at the moment of interview) were seen. In the two
cases where vice-chairmen were seen it seemed likely
that the chairmen were titular or at least 'distant'
from the main flow of the work. Though again the
majority of interviews were smoothly arranged, in
some cases some initial resistance was encountered
on the part of CEOs, who variously felt that their
chairmen would not know the answers, or that the CEO
knew them just as well, or that the chairman was
clearly too busy because he or she was difficult of
access even to the CEO. There were other causes of
difficulty in reaching the chairman or his
equivalent: one organisation had two changes of
chairman and a change of director during the 7 - 8
months which elapsed before the meeting could take
place; the chairman of another organisation had to
postpone two appointments because of bereavements in
the family, and that caused four months delay; and
in a third case first a rail strike, then a change
of secretary, then two further occasions when the
chairman decided suddenly to go away, postponed
three appointments made and caused seven months
delay. However it would be churlish to complain,
for this sort of assignment is not what chairmen
expect to undertake, some of them had heavy business
or professional commitments, and probably all of
them were very busy people. When the meetings did
take place they were, with the odd exception, very
forthcoming. The impression given by CEOs
separately was that nearly all of their chairmen
were adequately accessible to them, and some of them
were very involved in the week to week, if not day
to day, organisation of the work.

Interviews with CEOs all took place in the
offices (where they existed) of the organisations
concerned. The head office of BDA is in Carlisle,
though it was in the process of opening a sub-office
in London. Including this, twelve out of the
sixteen had offices in Central London or the City,
and the remaining four in inner suburb or rather
longer commuter range (Croydon and High Wycombe).

Of the twelve in inner London five were pressure
groups, probably wanting to be near the seats of
power; one (CHSA) is oriented to medical research
and might expect to gain by proximity to the BMA
complex in Tavistock Square; and one (CCE) serves
Greater London in the main. With the others, though
there were historical factors, the main attractions
of being central seemed to be convenience of access
by committee members and nearness to government
departments or professional advisers.

Those that were further out mostly emphasised
that it was less costly, and more convenient for
parking cars, though in most cases it was certainly
less convenient for those using public transport to
get to them. Arguments about recruitment of staff
in different types of location were not conclusive.

Little can be assumed about a visit to the
offices of voluntary organisations. They may be
approached down a gloomy side-street off a busy
shopping thoroughfare or found in the heart of a
residential area. They may occupy part of a
purpose-built office block, or a terrace house in
bed-sitter land: a property converted because it
has a preservation order on it, or one that is
waiting for the area to be redeveloped. They may
occupy a converted church or a converted factory.
All of these varieties were found within the sixteen
visited. All but three were reasonably convenient
of access by public transport.

Reception was in all cases adequate, though
sometimes only after having unexpectedly to ring the
front door bell. Inside, the immediate impressions
varied, some appearing rather cramped and others
quite spacious. They were generally reasonably
well, but far from luxuriously, appointed. The
greatest variety came in the rooms in which the
interview was conducted, generally the CEO's own
office but sometimes in the board room or a room
which combined the two functions. Leaving the
latter aside, at the one end of the scale one found
a large plush tycoon's office and a genteel drawing-
room: at the other, a room which had all the
appearances of a warehouse or temporary election
premises with trestle tables and stacked literature;
and the ante-room of a disorderly church hall, where
personal belongings littered the passages and the
room itself, and notices of old jumble sales adorned
the walls. These differences effectively epitomise
the different approaches found in the voluntary
sector. For some it is important to impress upon
those who come that the organisation is not poverty

stricken and that its chief officer is important and well-paid: for others the impression given, whether consciously or not, is of a gang of equals conducting an enthusiastic campaign. Most fall in between, adopting a modest posture and appearing to have a reasonably well organised office hierarchy.

The paid CEOs themselves were a varied group of people. Eleven were men, five women. Half were professional in the field specific to the organisation, and half were professional administrators. Three were retired officers of one of the fighting services. Generally they gave the impression of real commitment to their cause, that their work meant more to them than a means of earning a living. Almost without exception they were conservative in dress and appearance, and the only really long-haired CEO had a tie and suit on. Their relationships with their staff, in so far as this could be divined from two visits to the office, seemed universally good, and they were themselves reasonably relaxed and unhurried at interview, sometimes after a slight appearance of apprehension. This was so even in the cases when staff interrupted on some urgent matter or the CEO was having to double up as receptionist/office boy. CEOs were frank in their replies to questions, sometimes vouchsafing unprompted what they saw to be their own personal weakness or inadequacy: thus one felt a need for a better knowledge of staff management; another that his metier was professional rather than administrative. Most appeared vigorous though one gave the clear impression of being weary, particularly of the formalities imposed on staff relationships of recent years by employment legislation, and I was not surprised later to hear that he was just about to retire.

Chairmen too were varied. Nearly half of them had some professional or long-standing interest in the work. Not more than one third of them were retired persons, and these included an admiral and a senior civil servant. Those still in full time occupations included a barrister, MP, university professor, and shipowner. There was only one woman (of NAWCH) among them. In seven cases the chairman seemed to have an active initiating role; two of these were, as might have been expected, FNF and NGEC, where there was no paid CEO: in two cases it seemed likely that the role was being overplayed, and one was slightly sorry for the CEO. At the other end of the scale, there were two organisations where it seemed that the chairman was totally

passive, doing only what he was asked to do and
looking and thinking no further than the papers set
before him. In those cases one's anxiety was for
the organisation, for it must be too dependant upon
its staff and in certain circumstances could go
badly astray. In most cases chairmen gave congenial
and frank interviews and a few took unexpectedly
great time and trouble over them.

Interview guides were used both with CEOs and
with chairmen. In most cases information had been
obtained before interview, which helped save time
and aided quick understanding. The information so
requested, and the interview guides used, are set
out in Appendices D and E. The use of the guides
had to be modified to suit particular circumstances
- as when CEO and chairman were seen together, or
there was no office or paid CEO, and where certain
sections of the guide were not applicable in other
ways. On average almost two hours were spent on
each interview. In several cases supplementary
information had to be sought as the writing up of
the study exposed the needs, and organisations
showed themselves to be very willing to help in this
way.

This method of gathering information as a basis
for the project was felt to have been extremely
valuable, though its limitations will be clear to
anyone with experience of academic research. Viewed
as a broadening of the mind of the writer, rather
than the inescapable establishment of a total
description of the facts, it achieved what was
intended. It was followed by interviews with
government departments and others concerned with the
same sphere of activity, and these will be described
later. At this point it is now appropriate to
examine and discuss some of the more specific
findings about the organisations and fields of work
under review.

Chapter 3

ROLES AND RESOURCES

> ...there is a singular inability to achieve
> the right perspective on the contribution of
> the voluntary sector to social services: the
> contribution is either grossly exaggerated
> (lyrical paeans of praise) or seriously
> underestimated (the voluntary sector is simply
> an afterthought in service planning).
>
> - <u>Social</u> <u>Workers:</u> <u>their</u> <u>role</u> and <u>tasks.</u>
>   (<u>Barclay</u> <u>Report</u>)

The main chapters of this book will first describe
the work done by the organisations under review, and
the committees by whom they are controlled; then
their relationships with the other voluntary bodies
and with statutory organisations working in the same
fields. Accountability will have a discussion of
its own, and then in the final chapter it will be
possible to consider the future. In doing this we
shall take account not only of what organisations
are now doing, but also of how it looks to others,
e.g. in government or politics.

In this chapter the aim is to identify the
present contribution of the voluntary sector. As
has already been noted the ostensible objects of
each organisation, as quoted in official
publications, are set out in Appendix B. Here we
are concerned with what their current activities
are. Although the fields of activity of the
national organisations we are examining vary widely,
what are the <u>kinds</u> of things which they do? What
resources do they have to do them with? Are the
resources adequate for the work undertaken?

Information at our disposal should enable us to
answer these questions broadly, though subtleties
within the specialist services involved will no
doubt evade us: if for example, a voluntary
adoption agency is arranging an appreciable number
of adoptions each year this is a fact of the
present, illustrating a kind of role a national
organisation may undertake: but the question of
whether funds are likely to decline because the tide
of public opinion is running against adoption as
opposed to fostering, is a specialised assessment
which would not be within our study. The aim is to
describe the roles that are to be seen in the sector
as a whole, and the resources available to support

them, as an indication of what is possible and what
is not.

ROLES

So far as roles are concerned we shall be looking at
three main aspects. First, there is the provision
of personal services direct to individual clients, a
function which must in many respects be limited to
local representatives relating to people in their
localities: we shall be concerned only with
services provided directly by staff of the national
organisation, at head office or responsible directly
to head office. To illustrate by examples from
elsewhere, Barnardos' central organisation is
responsible for the provision of its residential
homes and of places in day care centres and would be
included: on the other hand, the home visitation
of the elderly undertaken by volunteers working with
local Age Concern organisations would not be
credited to Age Concern England.

The second aspect may be described as
'background services'. These may be of numerous
kinds - information for local groups, literature,
training etc. To illustrate again, if Age Concern
was under scrutiny, running courses for those
working in the Age Concern movement and for staff
from other organisations working with elderly
people, might be noted from its 1980/81 Annual
Report as one of its background services.

Third, there is the pressure group role, whose
respectability some organisations try to improve by
calling it 'social advocacy'. This may be the prime
function of the organisation, one that arises only
peripherally, or one amongst a number of equally
valuable functions: the National Federation of
Housing Associations, for example, provides expert
advice and information to its member associations,
but also campaigns on what it learns from them - as
it did in 1979 on the Care Needs of the Elderly and
other disabled groups, in housing association
sheltered and residential schemes.

There are other functions, such as research,
which could be separately listed, and will not be
overlooked in our analysis, but in the main the
three categories mentioned are convenient for a
start, and they are used in Table 3.1 which
summarises the chief functions referred to in
discussions with the organisations in the sample.
The lists do not claim to be comprehensive but
rather to indicate the main emphases of what the

Table 3.1: Chief Functions of Organisations in the Sample

| Organisation | Category of Function | | |
	Personal service direct to individual clients	Background services	Social advocacy
BDA	Holidays for 900 One residential home Some support in individual cases of injustice etc.	Video tapes on sign language Interpreters for meetings Development of visual telephone Advice/information to local branches (160) Journal Publications	Aims to change basic attitudes to deaf people
CHAR		Conferences Day training courses for members and others Publications for information of local groups and affiliated bodies	Press campaigns Submissions to committees of enquiry Parliamentary activity through All-Party Committee

CHSA	Volunteer stroke schemes (38) Welfare grants (£25,000) Postal counselling	Health education mainly via publications Conferences Grants for research work (£181,000) Support for local stroke clubs (202 affiliated)
CA	Homes and hostels (38) for: homeless, elderly, teenage mothers, boys in trouble Youth centres (6) Welfare work in prisons and with the armed services	
CCE	Information and advice especially on residential homes Financial help (£55,000 net)	
FNF	Walk-in Talk-in sessions	Support for local groups Conferences/lectures Newsletter Articles by members in press Submissions to committees of enquiry Parliamentary activity through All-Party Group

Table 3.1: (cont'd)

	Category of Function		
Organisation	Personal service direct to individual clients	Background services	Social advocacy
FEGH	Eleven residential homes Financial help (£134,000)		
HCT		Journal Conferences Study visits Library Bookshop	Response to government committees of enquiry or consultation documents
JGAD	Housing with care Two residential homes Holidays Employment at Craft Centre	Some information to schools etc.	
MHCAA	Adoption (26 cases) Counselling arising from adoption Two mother and baby homes and two children's homes, all in South Croydon		

MHA	Accommodation for retired people in nine historic houses		
NAWCH		Conferences Publications Library and information service	Press conferences Pressure in Whitehall and less so in Westminster Mostly at local Health Authority level
NGEC	Some personal advice to gypsies with problems	AGM/Conference Journal (annual) Articles in journals	Representations to Ministers and Civil Servants Comments on consult-ation documents Articles in journals
RADAR	Education and training for handicapped people Holidays	Conferences on special subjects e.g. speech impairment Designing aids to adapt work for handicapped Quarterly journal, bi-monthly newsletter and other publications 'Umbrella' organisation for 270 local bodies	Comments on draft government circulars and consultative documents Submissions to committees of enquiry Parliamentary activity through All-Party group

Table 3.1: (cont'd)

Organisation	Category of Function		
	Personal service direct to individual clients	Background services	Social advocacy
RBLHA	Housing for ex-service people		
Sh. H.& A.	Six residential establishments for children and young persons and for single parents and their children Floating school in London Adventure centre Day-care centre for under fives and their parents After-care for those leaving hostel Intermediate treatment cruises on Thames barge		

SHA   Support for local
       hostels for single
       homeless
       Grants/loans for
       furnishing
       Advice on fund
       raising

WEA   Back-up for adult
       education arranged
       locally by branches
       Twice-yearly WEA News

various bodies were doing at the time of interview. Figures in brackets are of amounts in the year.

A mere glance at the table is an immediate corrective to any who have been tempted to think in terms of voluntary bodies falling neatly into categories of service organisations, intermediate organisations, and pressure groups, corresponding to the three columns in the table. There are indeed seven which are listed only in the first column, and JGAD is so marginally in the column on background services as effectively to be an eighth service organisation: but thereafter the picture is less clear, and there are none appearing only in the third column, which might be expected of the 'pure' pressure group. Social advocacy in fact is always associated with background services, and sometimes with personal service as well. There are two organisations in the middle column alone, (SHA and WEA), in this table of main functions, though there is little doubt that they have influence that they bring to bear on social policy which would put them in the third column too; CHSA is firmly astride both personal and background services, but eschews social advocacy; BDA and RADAR certainly embrace all functions.

There is therefore no easy analytical way to take our examination of roles further, and it is proposed to do so first by looking at what appears in the three columns of the table, irrespective of whether the role referred to in each case is predominant or marginal to the organisation: but then to recognise that differences of emphasis or main intention must influence needs and resources, and to compare the situations within categories.

Personal Services

We look first at the column headed 'personal service direct to individual clients'. Perhaps it is not surprising that the most commonly mentioned role is the provision of residential care, homes all for special categories of person, - deaf, homeless, elderly, teenage mothers, boys in trouble, handicapped, deprived children. Running residential establishments like these today requires a variety of expertise - financial, property management, personnel management, social work, and a knowledge of the wider background of social policy and legislation. It requires a very considerable input of time at committee level, and also, if there is no substantial organisation behind it, at honorary

officer level. These are not resources which it can
be assumed will be available in every locality, or
available in the abundance that the number of
individual establishments might require. An
organisation able to draw upon resources from a
wider area, and/or to employ people to provide some
of the necessary expertise, is better placed.
Moreover, organisations of the sort in our list, by
definition have the 'urge' to do this work, and will
take steps to establish and encourage suitable local
provision.

Rented housing is less evidently a function
suitable for a national organisation. Some of the
expertise required is similar to that referred to
for residential homes, and more so perhaps than some
local associations appreciate, but demands made upon
those responsible are certainly much less, and it is
often important for there to be a knowledge of local
housing circumstances. It is significant that the
three organisations in our sample providing housing
are doing so for rather special reasons: JGAD
experimenting with housing for the disabled with
extra care 'built-in'; MHA accommodating retired
people whose financial and social backgrounds fit
them for occupying parts of historic country houses;
and RBLHA providing a special entree to rented
housing for elderly ex-service people who might not,
in the present shortage of such housing, get
priority from other sources.

The existence of SHA is a further commentary on
the world of 'voluntary housing'. Though not itself
directly initiating or providing accommodation, SHA
came into existence to provide technical backing for
hostels and housing schemes started locally (now 98
in number) but lacking expertise in the very complex
social and financial and legislative context in
which such schemes have to operate.

Holidays appear in the list three times, all
related to handicapped people. Again it is an
activity which can readily, perhaps even more
suitably, be undertaken by a national organisation,
which may have its own holiday accommodation
designed for the special needs of its clientele, or
may arrange holidays elsewhere after suitable
vetting of what is being offered and by
incorporating special travel arrangements.

The adoption service of MHCAA, though declining,
illustrates the appeal of a national service to
people whose religious beliefs are not widely
shared, but who are themselves scattered widely over
the country. One central organisation is able to

bring parties together who would otherwise find it
difficult.

One activity appearing several times in the
list of direct personal services is much less
obvious as a national function - that of
welfare work, counselling, advice or financial help
to individuals. The only extensive welfare work
seems to be that of the Church Army, and is mainly
in prisons and among members of the armed forces.
Full-time CA officers attached to establishments are
well placed to undertake this work, but casework is
undertaken also by CCE and FEGH and they do not have
locally based staff for it and this cannot on the
face of it be ideal. CCE has the equivalent of
eight whole-time caseworkers, and studiously avoids
undertaking any work which other statutory or
voluntary services are willing to do; it specialises
in advice on finding residential care, and much of
this can be done on the telephone; it operates
largely in the Greater London area; but even with
all these qualifications its closeness of contact
with its cases must often be tenuous. FEGH
financial help is substantially in one-off grants
for emergencies, where detailed knowledge might be
neither essential nor practicable even for a local
organisation; but it also makes some regular
allowances, and assessment of the need for these,
and the advice and consultation going with it, rests
with the one Case Secretary on the staff. It was
not therefore surprising to be told that she depends
largely on the advice of local social workers or
others.

CHSA is very straightforward in its policy on
these personal services. 'Counselling' there is,
but only in so far as it can be done by post:
welfare grants are made, but based solely on the
assessments made for them by Social Service
Departments. MHCAA counselling is limited to people
who have arranged adoptions through the society, and
Sh. H. & A. to after-care of those leaving their
hostels, so this work is limited and manageable by
comparison. Of the other bodies mentioning personal
service, BDA restricts itself to taking up a few
cases of injustice, apparently particularly in the
nature of test cases; and NGEC's advice to gypsies
seems very much to be on the basis of an
individual known to an individual ringing up for
advice. FNF has a different method to any, in its
'Walk-in Talk-in' sessions, held mainly in London,
and are group work rather than personal casework.
The limitations which inevitably have to be placed

by a national body in the casework which it can undertake are on this showing very varied.

These references by no means cover all that the organisations are doing by way of direct personal service. Some, such as the CHSA volunteer stroke schemes, are imaginative and innovative and, after a period of support from the national body, will depend for their future existence on adoption by local government or the local health authority. Others, like the employment which is offered by JGAD at its Craft Centre, can be little more than a pointer to others as to what might be done, rather than a significant quantitative contribution to 'employment', even for the disabled. RADAR is perhaps undertaking a little of both, providing both a pointer and a significant contribution, in its scheme for the education and training of handicapped people.

Background Services

We now turn to the second column in the table, on background services. These are provided by eleven bodies, only six of which have a significant number of local branches or affiliated organisations. There is 'advice' of all kinds, and support which is generally moral or given in kind, though is occasionally financial. Some of both is given via publications or special expertise. Background services may be special to the field of work, as epitomised by the BDA video tapes on sign language, the RADAR scheme for designing aids at work for the handicapped; or, in an administrative rather than a technological situation, by SHA assistance in negotiations between local hostels and the authorities concerned with hostel grants. Training courses, lectures or conferences for specialised workers fall into this category of activity, as do the grants for research work (mostly medical) which are made by CHSA.

Two organisations (HCT and NAWCH) make a point of offering library facilities for enquirers and research workers, though in both cases facilities are limited by the nature of the office accommodation. The subject of libraries is an important one and we shall be returning to it later in this chapter. HCT alone has a bookshop, again limited by space, but which it thinks to be important, on the grounds that it is prepared to obtain publications for customers of a nature most general bookshops would not be able to deal with.

Publications of one sort or another are produced by about half the organisations in the sample. Some of them have journals - notably HCT, BDA and RADAR. The HCT journal, Housing Review is by far the most substantial in its content. It is aimed at a general readership but assumes a knowledge and interest in housing affairs. It has a commentary on the housing scene, articles on policy and practical matters, reports, book reviews and correspondence. It is bi-monthly and costs £12 p.a. which includes HCT membership.

The BDA journal, The British Deaf News, is rather more inward-looking though it has some general articles around the subject of deafness. It is much more slender, and is also bi-monthly. It costs £2 p.a. RADAR's journal, Contact, is a quarterly. It is weightier in size, though not in content, even than Housing Review, because it is able to attract a great many advertisements: its content is largely practical, with articles, book reviews and correspondence, all aimed at disabled people. RADAR also has The Bulletin, monthly, with more ephemeral news. Like Contact it costs £2.50 p.a. Hope and Look Forward, the quarterly journals of CHSA, (each £1.00 p.a.) are aimed at those with chest, heart and stroke illnesses: they are small journals with no advertisements. Hope combines the journal function with that of giving news of the CHSA, and thus bridges the gap between the journals cited and the various newsletters which JGAD, CA, CHAR and NAWCH amongst others produce. These are largely for publicity purposes - aimed at the public - or for internal communication within the movement. The NAWCH quarterly newsletter, Update, is rather more than this, with conference reports and book reviews, as is WEA News, a twice yearly publication which is in newspaper format, but both are clearly aimed at their supporters.

It will be seen from what has been said that publications serve a number of different purposes. Though placed in the middle column of the table, they really straddle all three columns, for some of them are directed at the individual client: e.g.

'To smoke or not to smoke'   )
'Our client has asthma'   )   CHSA
'Breathing exercises for chronic   )
  bronchitis and emphysema'   )

'Your child in hospital:)
A parent's handbook'   )   NAWCH
'Your child in an immobilising   )
plaster'   )

Others are directed at those providing help for the
individual, and fall into the column on background
services: these are particularly the journals and
newsletters aimed at the movement, but also include
such publications as <u>Directory for the Disabled</u>, a
handbook of information and opportunities for the
disabled and handicapped people (RADAR), <u>Help to</u>
<u>give deaf people a hearing</u>, a BDA guide for the
legal profession, and <u>Supplementary Benefits for</u>
<u>Single Homeless People</u>, a CHAR guide. There is a
category of publication peculiar to organisations
with a large number of workers, paid or voluntary,
of which CA is the prime example, which provides
material assisting them with their work: and there
is extensive literature of the campaigning kind,
which falls into the 'social advocacy' column but
which sometimes overlaps with the background
information function: the CHAR Newsletter is an
example of this, as are some of CHAR's other
publications, e.g. <u>Monopoly of Misery</u>, a report on
Leicester's worst lodging houses.
     Only five of our sample produced a
comprehensive list of their publications (BDA, CHAR,
NAWCH, RADAR, WEA): except for CHAR's these show a
predominance of literature for the client or the
client's helper (it is difficult to draw a line
between these). About one-third of CHAR's
literature was information for local groups, and a
half seemed to be aimed at informing or influencing
the public. It is interesting to compare this
information with what is available in a catalogue of
the literature of other voluntary bodies.* A look
at the four with the longest lists of publications
is summarised in Table 3.2.
     It is clear that the advice and information
function of such organisations is a substantial one,
whether it be to clients direct or - more
appropriately for bodies such as CHAR and MENCAP -
to individuals and groups trying to help them.
Literature directed at changing legislation or

* Footnote

Campaign Books catalogue 1982/3. Campaign Books,
Huddersfield.

practice rarely comprises more than a third, and generally is much less.

Table 3.2: The targets of organisations' literature

Organisation	Publications directed at:					
	Client or Client's Helper		The Public		Those Making Policy	
	No.	%	No.	%	No.	%
Age Concern	34	66	7	13	11	21
MENCAP (Nat. Soc. for Mentally Handicapped Children and Adults)	28	80	7	20	–	–
MIND (Nat. Assn. for Mental Health)	20	36	15	27	20	36
Nat. Ccl. for One Parent Families	21	50	11	25	11	25

It will have become evident by this point that HCT is a different type of organisation from any other in the sample. As we have noted, its journal is of a different quality from any other, it alone offers a bookshop service, and almost alone it has library facilities for outside users. A glance at the third column of the table shows that it is not a militant pressure group, for its points of view are largely made within its journal or in response to government documents. Partly this different approach arises from the field it covers, housing, an enormous subject on which policies rather than postures are called for: but this does not explain it entirely. HCT epitomises a kind of voluntary organisation, probably paralleled by the National Children's Bureau or the Centre for Policy on Ageing, a body aimed at study, information or research, exerting influence more by letting hard facts seep into public thinking than by pushing them at politicians.

Social Advocacy

We may now look at the functions listed in the final
column of the table, under the heading 'social
advocacy', by which we largely think of pursuing
causes in the corridors of power. We have already
touched on some of these in passing, the production
of publications in particular, but there are others,
and patterns of practice may be seen by a look at
the list. The most commonly mentioned are
submissions to committees of enquiry, such as Royal
Commissions or the Barclay Committee of the National
Institute for Social Work on the role and tasks of
social workers; response to consultative documents,
such as the DHSS Green Paper on financing services
for the mentally handicapped in 1981; or uninvited
comments on official reports which relate to the
organisation's work such as the NAWCH response to a
Nursery Nurse Examination Board Report. Other
representations are also made in Whitehall, mostly
on the initiative of the voluntary organisation,
though RADAR is invited by government departments to
comment on draft circulars to local or other
authorities (though these were relatively few in
number during the era of the Conservative government
of 1979-83). These activities bear closely on the
wider working relationship between voluntary and
statutory bodies, and this will be discussed more
fully in a later chapter.
     Press and Parliament both have a full share of
attention. Press campaigns - articles, press
releases, press conferences - are mentioned by
several of our sample. The press is the vehicle for
those wishing to influence public opinion, either as
part of an attack on a political or administrative
issue, or in order to seek other changes in public
opinion. The BDA, for example, was beginning a
period in which it declared an aim of changing
general attitudes to the deaf, though it was not at
the stage of being specific about the methods of
doing so.
     Parliamentary activity in three of the five
organisations mentioning it was largely through an
All-Party Group, and this highlights the very strong
impression given in the interviews with CEOs and
chairmen that their organisations were not party-
oriented, the issues with which they were concerned
were largely not tangled with party ideologies: the
All-Party Group was a natural vehicle for their
representations to politicians and its importance
was clear. Presumably the House of Commons Select

Committee on Social Services will also offer similar
opportunities at times. At Government, as opposed
to Parliamentary, level, representations were
especially to the Minister(s) most relevant to the
organisations' field(s) of work.

NAWCH was unusual in having to address itself
on many issues to District Health Authorities,
exerting pressure there often with the implicit if
not explicit support of the DHSS. The situation was
most nearly parallelled by CHAR, making
representations to local authorities with the
approval of DoE, but in their case the work was more
often done by local groups or member organisations.

From this brief summary of social advocacy
functions it becomes clear that, despite the fact
that no organisation is found in that category alone,
there are five of our sample largely concerned with
public policy on one aspect or another, to the
virtual exclusion of personal service to clients.
These are the 'pressure groups' in our sample. They
are CHAR, FNF, HCT, NAWCH and NGEC. The fact that
others have a pressure group role as well, notably
RADAR, does not invalidate the conclusion, and at
certain stages in this chapter, when we look at
resources, we shall need to separate our examination
of the five from the remaining thirteen which we may
describe as service organisations. The emphases of
the two types are so different that the resources
they may require must also be different.

RESOURCES

By 'resources' we are not thinking only of financial
support, vital though this is. The Concise Oxford
Dictionary defines resources as 'stock that can be
drawn on', and this also includes stocks of ideas,
information and manpower. Unless all of these are
adequate the work will be that much less valuable or
effective. There is however nothing precise about
'adequacy' and all that we can do here is to
describe what resources are, and relate them to the
work which the organisation is electing to do at the
present time, and to what it may indicate it would
like to be doing in the near future. From this
certain conclusions as to adequacy will be apparent,
as will conclusions or reflections on a number of
other matters.

Sources of ideas are variable, and are almost
as difficult to identify as such intangibles as
inspiration and enthusiasm. The main impression is
that ideas and policies emanate from committees and

staff, though in certain organisations grass-roots influence is also great. BDA , for example, has an annual conference and a triennial congress where, it reports, there is 'no shortage of ideas'. WEA gets much inspiration from its districts. HCT, with a substantial number of conferences always being organised, gets a steady generation of ideas that way, though their development is handicapped by the organisation's struggle just to keep alive. NAWCH has an annual conference which is 'packed out', and provides material with which the committee can make policy.

We shall in this section of this chapter look first at staff, and go on to an examination of information and finance. The chapter that follows will discuss committees.

Staff

To what extent are the organisations in our sample served by well qualified staff? Here it has to be made plain that any conclusions must be extremely tentative. All sorts of questions which are ultimately unanswerable arise. For example, what does 'well qualified' mean? Paper qualifications have some relevance for certain functions, e.g. in housing management, social work or medicine: but what are suitable qualifications for organising holidays? And how does one judge the wisdom of those who insist that in-service training is better than anything else, as for example does CCE in its recruitment of caseworkers?

Secondly, what assessment can be made of the adequacy of the numbers of staff available for particular work, whether senior staff with specified roles and/or paper qualifications, or supporting staff without which their efforts might be diluted, handicapped or frustrated? Without an intimate knowledge of the work and staff structure, which this study has not attempted, there can be no conclusive assessment of this sort.

Nevertheless something must be attempted, if only to point the way to further and more precise study by readers concerned with particular organisations, or by those who may be able to plan further research. As a beginning Table 3.3 has been drawn up. It shows, for service organisations only, the main functions drawn from the earlier Table 3.1 which would seem to call for specialist staff, and the staff known to be available particularly for these functions. It shows that with one notable

exception, residential care, there are in most cases
specially appointed or suitably qualified officers
for each of the major functions of the organisations.

Table 3.3: Staff functions and specialist staff
available

Organisation	Functions	Staff
BDA	Holidays Technical development Publications	Sports and leisure officer Communication and Interpreting services officer; Video editor; Education officer; Editor (Publications)
CHSA	Medical advice and expertise Publications	Director General is medically qualified Editor
CA	Residential care Social work	Director of Residential Social Work Services Assistant Chief Secretary (Social work)
CCE	Social work	Casework Director and casework staff
FEGH	Residential care Social work	Executive staff qualified or experienced in domestic science, nursing, estate management and social work
JGAD	Residential care and housing Holidays	
MHCAA	Social work Residential care	Social worker, with case, adoption, medical and psychiatric, social work and legal advisers

MHA	Property management	CEO quals are ASCA, MBIM
RADAR	Holidays Technical development	Holiday officer National and regional organisers with spec- ialist panel of advisers
	Publications	Publications officer
RBLHA	Housing management and development	
Sh. H & A	Residential care Social work	Social work secretary and full-time after- care secretary
SHA	Housing administration Social work	CEO is M. Phil. MBIM Secretary is MIH Development Manager is RICS, MIH
WEA	Educational knowledge Educational administration	Relevant staff are largely in the field

The two organisations which do not measure up to this are JGAD and RBLHA. JGAD has no officials designated to deal with residential care, housing or holidays: of this it should be said that JGAD has its own separately constituted housing association, whose staff are no doubt available to advise, but this was not separately examined. As to RBLHA, it was stated at interview that all staff are drawn from the services and none have housing qualifications.

The situation concerning residential care is significant. The Church Army alone designates an officer in charge of it; others with much activity in this direction, like FEGH and MHCAA, do not. This seems to indicate that the function is not generally thought to require specialist supervision. It is regarded as a general administrative or management function. This attitude will add fuel to the flames of a controversy already burning brightly, which is whether residential social work and the roles of care staff are of the same status and degree of speciality as social work in the community, and what is involved in good quality administration of residential homes.

The Barclay committee on the role of social workers noted with concern that 'over 80 per cent of residential staff have received no relevant training', indicating apparently that residential care deserved higher status: though this did not go far enough for Professor Olive Stevenson, who commented that "it is a pity that they did not begin the report with the same useful account of what residential and day care social workers do as they gave for field workers".(1) The staff designations in our table appear at most to epitomise a somewhat lukewarm or hesitant approach to giving residential care a status of equal importance to community social work or even to the organisation of holidays.

The main link between staff and committee is the CEO, though there may be several other links via senior officers attending main committees or serving subcommittees. The sort of relationships the CEO forges, the sort of lead he is able to give, are clearly of vital importance to the organisation.

A first impression of CEOs seen has been described on page 44. They did not in the main answer the description made by Mullin of the staff of charities:

> It is a confirmed habit amongst too many charities to hire retired men with pensions – drawing on such grateful bodies as the Officers Association – for their staff vacancies. This way they achieve dutiful obedience, safety against risk-taking, and an eternal supplement (through index-linked pensions) to meagre salaries.(2)

Only three of those interviewed in our sample were retired officers of one of the fighting services, and the more significant first impression was that half were professional in the field specific to the organisation, and the other half (if we include the three officers) were professional administrators.

There has been a subtle change of emphasis in the role of the CEO during the last 10 - 15 years, and it is epitomised by the change of designation in many organisations from Secretary to Director. The Secretary was indeed what the Concise Oxford Dictionary says: an official appointed by the society 'to conduct its correspondence, keep its records, and deal in the first instance with its business'. He was acting on behalf of his committee. The better secretaries assisted the committee by providing it with advice and information prior to its making decisions on important matters, and saved it some work by extending the 'dealing in the first instance' to dealing once and for all with minor matters which came to the organisation. The welfare state, however, became more complex and comprehensive: the interests of voluntary organisations became of themselves more specialised as groups pressed for attention to particular social conditions, personal handicaps or types of illness or infirmity. It was important to keep abreast of developments in government policy or in professional practice. Committees could not of themselves cover all the matters which came to them, secretaries had to become more knowledgeable in sociological, social work, social administration, medical and other fields, and when resources made it possible they had to recruit staff to help them give adequate service to the committees. Not only were they expected to do this, but they had to represent the organisation in discussions with government departments or other voluntary bodies, or take part in committees or public debates on matters with which their organisations were concerned. It was therefore often a recognition of a larger role, as well as a matter of giving status and avoiding confusion with the shorthand-typist, that made many organisations change the name from Secretary to Director.

Of recent years there has also been the major impact of the employment legislation of the 1970s, with which often came moves to unionise the staff of voluntary organisations. As the journal of the National Council of Voluntary Organisations put it in 1981:(3) 'By and large, the staff in both charitable and non-charitable voluntary organisa-tions are better trained, younger and more career-oriented' and in some, though by no means all, of these organisations such staff thought almost as a matter of course in terms of trade union membership being a necessity. They must at times have felt well-justified, for as the same article puts it,

It is still not uncommon in small organisations for the newly-formed union's first discovery to be that its members have no signed contracts of employment at all, often because the employers have relied on goodwill and informality to the degree they have contravened the employment laws.

'Goodwill and informality', a sense of commitment to a cause – which often undoubtedly led to a lack of concern about whether salaries were as good as those next door – did describe the functioning of many even national voluntary bodies before 1970. Several of the CEOs who were interviewed harked back nostalgically to those days, not so much because life was easier for them then – though this was so – but because they deplored the amount of time they now have to spend on employee relations, sometimes seemingly pointless formalities, to the detriment of the 'real work' of the organisation with which they are generally closely and personally identified. This is another aspect on which special knowledge is now required, and the CEO with anything more than a handful of staff has been in difficulty because he has not generally had skills and experience in personnel management of this sort, as several of those interviewed made plain: and in most organisations he has felt that he had to take personal responsibility for it, and that the organisation in any case could not justify the appointment of a special person to do so. Yet even with a staff of only 20, staff consultation, complaints procedures, terms and conditions of appointment, health and safety at work, let alone superannuation and 'staff welfare', add up to an appreciable responsibility. Sometimes some of it falls almost by chance on another member of staff, notably the accountant, or the company secretary if there is one, but this may be even less satisfactory for they may have no more special knowledge than the Director and possibly less concern.*

It is not only the Director of the voluntary organisation that has found the work changing. An article on local authority Directors of Social Services in 1983 (4) was entitled 'It's a totally different job now'. Amongst the requirements of the job referred to were acting as the local authority's professional social services adviser, and answering questions from elected members when defending a particular SSD policy, and some directors were

* Footnote

It is good to be able to add that the NCVO now offers an advisory service on these matters.

quoted as estimating that up to 40% of their time was spent on industrial relations and trade union matters. Again, there are calls for 'more investment in management training'. The article commented:

> There is little doubt that social work has been going through one of its biggest ever upheavals in top management. Last year at least 12 directors resigned and many new appointments have been made, often of relatively young people. Many of these resignations were of people who had opted for early retirement and it is legitimate to speculate that increasing pressures were at least partly the cause.

The CEO of a voluntary organisation is far from being the equivalent of a civil servant. Though he is generally wise to appear party-politically neutral, he has the duty <u>not</u> to be neutral in his attitude to particular issues: certainly he takes a part in public debate in a way no civil servant would be expected to do. He has to stand for the policies he has often promoted within the organisation; he cannot remain anonymous and leave it to the politician or even - perhaps the equivalent in the voluntary sphere - his chairman. He has personally to provide the technical expertise on some of the issues with which his committee deals, for he is unlikely to have a full range of specialist staff to support him, which the civil servant can perhaps reasonably expect. He has personal responsibility for the management of the staff and the administration of the organisation.

The CEO's position is nearer to that of the Managing Director of a company, but different in that he is not on the board. In only one of the sample organisations (RBLHA) had that been the case and it was about to be altered. The CEO and supporting staff are expected to prepare papers on main issues for the committee, providing information on which it can make judgements, and to have put their recommendations, if they have them, in the paper or when initiating discussion: thereafter they are expected to revert to a more neutral position whilst the committee decides. The CEO has therefore a particularly and uniquely middle-man role which is not always appreciated either by committee on the one side or staff on the other. He has the duty of representing the staff position to the committee and the committee to the staff: of

being the servant of the committee with a real
loyalty to its decisions, having to take some of the
knocks for its decisions both inside and outside the
office yet maintaining a consistency and integrity
of policy and administration for the organisation.
He is fortunate if he has even one colleague with
whom he can share his thoughts entirely: his may
therefore be a lonely role.

A century ago, even half a century ago, there
were prima donnas in the voluntary movements. Such
names as Dr. Barnardo, Margery Fry, and Octavia Hill
spring readily to mind, or William Carlisle, founder
of the Church Army. They were amateurs, pioneers
and often autocrats. Today prima donnas are few and
far between, though voluntary organisations tend to
attract some who aspire to such a role. Today the
real leaders have to be technocrats and democrats,
and pioneering plays a smaller part, though we
shall discuss this matter again later in this book.
The impression formed at interviews of all the CEOs
in our sample was of a body of men and women doing
the work they had to do with real commitment. That
they may be subject to certain restrictions is a
matter which becomes apparent as our study
continues, but that their personal calibre is high
there seems no doubt.

It is a favourite sport amongst the less
thoughtful of journalists and politicians to 'knock'
the expenditure of any social welfare organisation,
statutory or voluntary, on staff. It is the
implicit assumption that paid staff are parasites on
the organisation, taking money which could and
should be used for direct assistance of needy
people: that the best organisation is one whose
salary levels are low but dedication high; which
spends nothing on administration but is nevertheless
a model of efficiency, which does not undertake
research into the causes of distress but gives the
money instead to ameliorate its symptoms; or in
short, that soup kitchens always still get the
popular vote. For this reason, perhaps, voluntary
organisations generally, and certainly most of those
in the sample, do not make plain in their accounts
how much is spent on staff salaries, knowing that
the information may be used out of context: and
indeed, such a figure is meaningless without the
knowledge of what the people who receive salaries
are paid to do. Nevertheless, some attempt to make
comparison between the organisations in the sample
seemed worth attempting, and the details of this
comparison are described in Appendix F.

Tentatively one might conclude from it that the use of the ratio of expenditure on essential administration per head of staff has some useful validity if carefully applied. If, for example, the work of an organisation consists largely in the personal service of its specialist staff, with little pure administration, as in the casework of CCE, the ratio will be lower than in cases where considerable administrative expenditure is involved, as in the organisation of conferences or the production of publications.

Information

Neither staff nor committee can function adequately when their decisions are not based on sound facts. Management and administration require facts generated within the organisation: the study did not cover this, though several of those seen vouchsafed of their own accord that their organisation was weak on recording its own work. Decisions on wider policy involve a knowledge of the 'field' in which the organisation works - housing, child care, education, etc. - at levels which may include government legislation or policy making, academic thinking in particular disciplines, local authority responsibilities, the contributions of other voluntary organisations, the views of the consumer or client. It is important that any organisation today should be aware of and responsive to this wider context of its work, and the study therefore raised questions aimed at establishing how far this was so.

At this point a clear division arises between the service organisations and the pressure groups. So far as the first are concerned the answer to the question 'Is information collected systematically?' was a hardly qualified 'no' in all cases but that of RADAR. This is directly comparable to the findings of Kramer's cross-national study of agencies serving the physically and mentally handicapped, which were that in England 'only two of the (20) agencies have an information system or publish service statistics'. (5) So far as the five pressure groups are concerned the answer was more positive, and will be described shortly.

The conclusion about service organisations is not however that they are all ill-informed. A supplementary question was aimed at finding out what information reached the organisation, i.e. on what sources of knowledge it might be assumed policy and

practice were based. Here the response was better,
though varied. At the one extreme there is the
emphasis on what is in people's heads or received
into the ordinary filing system. One should not
belittle this, but it is obvious that it is not
totally reliable and is difficult of retrieval.
FEGH was one example: it depended on its Case
Secretary to acquire knowledge about sources and
regulations relating to aid to individuals, and did
not feel any need for an information input in the
process of running residential homes, though was
just about to subscribe to its first journal,
Community Care. Near to this came MHA, which
depended largely on what it was told by DoE and its
own architect; and WEA which had an Education
Advisory Committee whose members were assumed to be
well-versed from their own sources to advise on
policy. Some depended considerably on other
organisations, mostly from intermediary bodies such
as NCVO or NCVCCO, NACRO and NFHA: when these were
spoken of it was with real appreciation and their
information function is clearly highlighted as
important.

Many service organisations take journals, some
only one or two (CCE for example depends on New Age
and Choice, and RBLHA takes only the housing
journals) and others expansively stated that they
took every journal going. This latter claim must be
taken in context, but the context, for example, of
RADAR or SHA is wide if all aspects or subjects
relating to disability or homelessness are to be
covered. A detailed count of what journals the
sample organisations took was not made, but there is
little doubt that Community Care was the most
popular in the social service field. It seems
likely that the position described by Streatfield
and Wilson in their study of information in local
authority Social Services Departments (6) would be
mirrored in these voluntary bodies, namely that
journals seen most regularly were, by frequency of
citation:

Community Care	73%
Social Work Today	62%
New Society	43%
Social Services	38%
(now ceased publication)	

Some referred to conferences and seminars,
though this was often qualified: with a large staff
like CA a wide coverage of conferences can be

achieved, but others have to be very selective for
the process can be very time consuming. Government
departments were a source of information to one or
two only.

Research and intelligence played a part in
various ways, but only for four of the thirteen.
Only RADAR had its own Intelligence staff, working
on such subjects as the availability of facilities
for the disabled, though CA said that it once had a
full-time research officer, but no longer. Funds
were made available from time to time to facilitate
research by university departments, by BDA, CHSA,
JGAD and RADAR, on subjects closely related to the
work they were doing e.g. the relative costs of
types of institutional care. There was notably
little study of consumer views, 'notably' because
more than half of the thirteen had no
consumer/client input elsewhere: BDA and RADAR are
exceptions, and JGAD, MHCAA and WEA also have
'consumers' on their committees.

Particular notice was taken of whether the
organisations had libraries of their own. The
answer was 'yes' in only five of the service
organisations, if one includes in that the 'shelf of
books' available in the SHA office. Even these were
very varied. Largely they consisted of items to be
borrowed and indeed there was generally little
encouragement to read in 'the library' itself: a
chair and a small table might be available but the
room might be unattractive and cold. RADAR and WEA
made it available to outside enquiries, but the WEA
library though substantial, is now largely an
archive, not kept up to date at all, on the grounds
that those wanting educational information can
readily obtain it in university libraries.
Classification in all cases is ad hoc if it exists
at all, (though RADAR has adopted the King's Fund
Centre classification), and at best the library is
overseen part-time by a member of staff who has
other responsibilities too. Subjects covered are
always near to the purposes of the organisation -
social work and Christian for CA; diseases relevant
to disablement for JGAD. All the libraries are
quite small, in no case but WEA's exceeding 100ft
of shelving, and generally considerably less.

In the work already quoted, by Streatfield and
Wilson, the authors say: 'It will be obvious by now
that we hold a rather jaundiced view of social
services departmental libraries'. 'The overall
level of staffing and equipping ... reflects the
low priority being given to formal provision of

information in general and externally produced
material in particular'. (7) There seems every
reason to make the same comment about most of the
voluntary service organisation libraries, RADAR
perhaps excepted. Some defended the position by
explaining that it was too expensive to maintain a
library, and at first thought this seems to be a
valid argument where organisations have a limited
field of operation, such as CCE, MHCAA, Sh. H & A
or the housing associations. It might be argued
that the cost of a library would take too much from
limited funds, and that information is best obtained
from the umbrella bodies some mentioned, such as
NCVCCO or NFHA. A second thought however would
question this contention: for the very fact of
their limited field of operation means that the
essential expenditure would be relatively small,
(indeed SHA's 'shelf of books' epitomises it) if
kept to a scale which aimed at providing a service
to their staff which kept them up to date and
efficient. To achieve this adequately really means
to have the resources on the spot, not in some
remote 'intermediary' or university place some
miles, or tens of miles away.

Other bodies may defend the absence of a
library or adequate information system by reference
to the quality of their advisers - as would CHSA and
WEA - but professionalism by proxy cannot be very
satisfactory for staff who want to play a
significant part in the work.

For bodies like BDA, CA and RADAR with
extensive coverage, a good library of their own
seems essential. None of them, it seems, now really
live up to the standard which their responsibilities
surely demand of them.

We must now return to a look at the information
bases of the pressure groups. That this matter is
even more important in their case than in that of
the service organisations is clear. As CHAR put it:
'Our whole work is about fact-finding'. In their
study of the influences bearing on policy decisions
in a number of case studies, Hall et al concluded:
'First, there is the question of the authority of
the facts. The more authoritative they are seen to
be the more potentially influential': and later,
'the mere existence of facts about an issue may have
little impact unless, literally, they are discussed
and used'. (8)

The two pressure groups without paid staff (FNF
and NGEC) were inevitably dependent for their fact
finding and fact using on individual members, re-

inforced from time to time by committee action.
They had one big advantage in that they had
'consumers' well (perhaps over-well?) represented on
their committees. Individual members who were
academics were especially well-placed to obtain
information, but others were able to do so partly,
in the case of FNF, through the <u>Law and Social Work
Journal</u>, and through another voluntary organisation,
Campaign for Justice in Divorce; and in the case of
NGEC, partly from the Department of the Environment
and the Department of Education and Science.

These bodies' activities have a more homespun
look to them by comparison even with small
organisations such as CHAR, NAWCH and HCT. With all
of these the assembly of information is notably
systematic. They all have libraries: CHAR has
about 50ft of shelving in a room used for several
other purposes; its subjects housing, alcoholism,
mental health, vagrancy etc. all relating to
homeless single people, mostly in topical
publications. It is used almost entirely by its
staff.

NAWCH has a larger library, perhaps 100ft of
shelving, again in an all-purpose room. Subjects
include health, health services, and children.
Material has been collected over many years, and
NAWCH obtained a grant from the Charities Aid
Foundation recently to enable it to employ an
Information Officer who is organising it into a more
readily usable form. It has its own classification
system, with a thesaurus, and is used not only by
staff but also by members of the public, government
officials and research workers. It spent £300 in
1981 on acquisitions. NAWCH not only acquires
publications and other documents, but collects its
own information on local policies and consumer
views, information which it maintains would 'not be
so frank' if obtained by statutory bodies.

The library at HCT is as large if not larger,
with over 10,000 items. Its subjects are planning,
housing management and policy, and design and
construction, and it is classified under these three
headings. With a very small staff keeping an index
up to date has proved difficult, but assistance in
selecting material sought is readily available, and
the library is used by enquirers, particularly from
universities. It has certain historical and other
material not easily obtainable, if at all, from any
other library. It participates in the inter-library
(specialist libraries) loans scheme. It is an
important part of the study and discussion functions

which the Trust aims to provide.

Staff in these three organisations must keep abreast of developments and thinking in their fields of activity. Publications and conferences play a part, though HCT staff have no time to attend conferences other than those they themselves organise, but as these are extensive and of wide coverage of subject this is probably no great handicap. NAWCH alone feels able to initiate research of a more rigorous kind, not from its own funds but by obtaining grants from elsewhere: examples are of a 3 year research project at Kingston Polytechnic, funded by the King Edward's Hospital Fund, on educational material preparing children for hospital; and a 2 year project on teaching in hospital, undertaken with a grant from the Leverhulme Trust.

In sum, it may be said that the pressure groups seem to be fully seized of the need to be well-informed, and are probably leaders in their chosen subjects. The extent to which their information is available to others is rather variable; improvements in classification and facilities for the outside enquirer could be made.

Finance

'Money is the root of all evil', ran the words of the song now forgotten perhaps by all but older readers. It is also the root of all activity, or nearly all of it, by voluntary organisations. The very smallest no doubt manage for a while on the honorary work and uncharged expenses of eager members, and much credit is due to these supporters: but even FNF, which could not produce the statement of accounts requested, knew that it wanted money and sought advice on how best to obtain it. It should therefore be a worthwhile exercise to see how the 'big boys', and those who have been going for many years, manage to pay for what they are doing. To do so an examination of their accounts should be the main source of information.

On the statements of accounts of voluntary organisations in the sample the layman in financial matters might reasonably be excused for thinking that the intention was to disguise rather than make plain the facts of the situation. One looks in vain for any uniformity of treatment, any consensus on what headings of income or expenditure should be. Whether or not investments are a source of income or separately accounted for; whether activities which generate income should have two gross figures, possibly merged with others, on both sides of the account, or appear in one place as a net figure: what the distinctions are between subscriptions, donations and grants, and whether they should be shown separately or in one lump; whether completely to obliterate items of expenditure on salaries or fund-raising; are but a few examples of the questions the enquirer becomes painfully conscious have not been agreed in the world of voluntary bodies and/or their treasurers and accountants. No doubt there are all sorts of traditions within the organisations, practical difficulties and professional arguments why uniformity is undesirable and understandability is not achieved. This does not invalidate the point, and it was gratifying, if not satisfying, to find that certain of those interviewed agreed with it.*

A fair amount of 'doctoring' had therefore to be done to make reasonable comparison between the finances of the organisations in the sample. If individual bodies do not recognise the figures that follow in Table 3.4 they are asked to bear in mind the strictures just made, the fact that every effort has been made to make a fair job of it, and in particular that, as in the whole of this study, the object is not mainly to comment on individual cases but to draw broad conclusions across the board.

It was clear that income falls for these organisations into four main categories - donations and subscriptions, interest and dividends, government grants, and legacies. A category for 'trading' is not included, because only in two cases (listed in the note below the table) might it have been relevant. Organisations do not make a profit for general purposes out of rents, or fees for residential care: in the two cases referred to there is a 'net income' from publications, though whether it could rightly be described as profit after staff and other overhead costs had been allowed for is very doubtful.

Income from legacies was a very variable figure, and it was clear that a conclusion from one year's accounts could be misleading. Figures were

* Footnote

The Accounting Standards Committee has (1984) published a discussion paper, Accounting by Charities, which touches on some of these points.

Table 3.4: Income for General Purposes

Organis-ation	Total income for general purposes (excluding legacies) £000s	Donations and sub-scriptions £000s	Interest and dividends £000s	Government grants £000s	Surplus/deficit in year £000s	Legacies received in year £000s
BDA	125	94	31	–	–96	126
%	100	75	25			
CHAR	76	14	2	53	3	–
%	100	18	3	70		
CHSA	477	263 (1)	123	–	–127	410
%	100	55	26			
CA	767	367	400	–	–805	463
%	100	48	52			
CCE	139	120 (2)	16	–	1	1
%	100	86	12			
FNF	2	2	–	–	–	–
%	100	100				
FEGH	249	87	134	–	–214	125
%	100	35	54			
HCT	52	22	3	–	–1	–
%	100	42	6			
JGAD	210	76	119	–	–96	293
%	100	36	57			

MHCAA	90	52	36	–	–5	30
%	100	58	40	–		
MHA	126	15	111		5	–
%	100	12	88			
NAWCH	55	7	3	41	9	–
%	100	13	5	75		87
RADAR	496	143	36	205	88	87
%	100	29	7	41		
Sh.H&A	185	84	101	–	–109	66
%	100	45	55		–2	
WEA	91	41	7	39	–2	1
%	100	45	8	43		

Other significant income not included in this table was:

CHSA	Surplus on sale of investments	£87,000
FEGH	Profit on sale of investments	£28,000
HCT	Net income from publications, conferences and meetings	£27,000
RADAR	Net income from publications	£86,000

(1) Includes some small ad hoc grants for work done.
(2) Includes some "grants".

therefore prepared of the first three items, and of
the surplus or deficit before any account was taken
of the legacies. All the organisations were
included except RBLHA and SHA whose almost total
involvement in the use of public money made
available to housing associations put them in quite
a different financial category; and NGEC whose
figures were too small to give adequate significance
to a breakdown. Figures were prepared for total
income for general purposes only, excluding for
example the results of appeals related to specific
projects, or of government grants likewise; and
categories of income were expressed as percentages
of this. A final column shows the legacies received
in the year under examination. Table 3.4 sets out
the results.

When Dame Eileen Younghusband described
voluntary organisations related to social work, in
1975, she wrote: 'Practically all voluntary
organisations of standing in the social services
field were grant-aided from public funds in the
1970s'. Our sample shows that this was not so, so
far as general funds are concerned. Only RADAR
of 'social services' organisations received such a
grant and that amounts to 41% of general income.
RADAR also received grants for thirteen specific
purposes (not shown in the table), as did BDA from
DHSS for training volunteers: CHSA for the
Volunteer Stroke Schemes: and CA for work with HM
Forces: but none of these impress one as adequate
corroboration for the Younghusband assertion.

Information provided by government departments
in answer to Parliamentary Questions in 1982/3
listed 75 organisations, in the population of 150
from which our sample was taken, which were getting
government grants; but again many of these grants
were for specific projects for specific periods and
not to help with general expenses. Unfortunately
the answers did not distinguish between them, but it
is clear from this as from our own enquiries that
considerable work is done with no government grants
whatsoever.

This finding is much more in line with Kramer
than with Younghusband. Kramer found that

only one of the twenty agencies in the sample
reported as much as nine per cent of its income
from central government, and then grants
constituted less than 2 per cent of the income
of the other five agencies receiving such
funds.

On the other side of the coin, it is remarkable that two pressure groups top the table of government grants, in the percentages of income that come from this source, and in both cases are well over 50%. CHAR was started by government, and is to some extent its secret weapon against local autorities, though undoubtedly central government also finds the weapon used against it too. NAWCH specifically states that 'Each year (it) receives a DHSS grant towards (its) work of persuading hospitals to implement government policy'. Yet HCT struggles along on a shoe-string, getting nothing in this way; 'entirely independent of any grant from government ... independence is very precious to us; it is also very expensive' says its report.

Organisations with more than half their income from interest and dividends are mostly long-established: CA 1882, FEGH 1905, JGAD 1866, Sh. H & A 1843 - only MHA 1955 being the exception. Are they coasting along, comfortably living within their 'unearned income', unchallenged by needs to persuade others that they are measuring up to modern standards of activity? Three out of four of the 'oldies' certainly give quite the opposite impression: CA was appealing vigorously, in an attempt to 'balance the books' by 1982 - 'the income of CA can no longer depend on the generosity of the rich and the dead' wrote the CEO in 1980. It had just had a radical examination of the way its organisation was working, and had ideas for new work departures if resources could be found for them.

JGAD has an active appeal organisation, given an additional boost by the 1981 International Year of Disabled People, of which year the Annual Report wrote: 'income from donations and legacies reached the budgeted target and is over £50,000 higher than 1980, though the increase was barely sufficient to cover the effect of inflation'. Sh. H & A had a complete review of work and management in 1972 which pointed to a need to modernise ideas, and which seems to have been well implemented, and work has expanded. It admits to relying more on legacies than subscriptions, and to having both 'hawks' and 'doves' in its committee - the former wondering where the money is to come from, and the latter tending to the belief that if good work is done money will come from somewhere to pay for it. One source of income is constantly being complained about as being inadequate - receipts from the provision of residential care, mainly because it was not used as much by local authorities for placements

as previously. Five of the sample were probably
losing appreciable sums of money because of
authorities cutting back on the use of homes other
than their own.

The final two columns of the table show that
without legacies many organisations would be in
severe financial difficulty, though just how
important legacies are cannot be fairly judged on
one year. The annual report of FEGH, for example,
stated that legacies and donations were down £89,000
on the previous year. Organisations varied in the
use to which legacies were put. Some treated them
as income in the accounts (BDA, CA, FEGH, MHCAA,
RADAR) though RADAR, for example, transferred the
total received from legacies, plus the further
substantial amount of £56,000, to the General Fund
in the year under review. Others met the year's
deficit out of legacies and put the balance to an
accumulated fund (CHSA, ShH&A) or capital reserve
(CCE). Interest and dividends appear, as the table
shows, in all cases but one (FNF), and presumably
arise from such transfers, either of legacies, or of
excess of income over expenditure perhaps caused by
legacies. Whatever the nominal difference in the
application of legacies it seems that in the end
they are generally used if necessary to meet
deficits but put into investments if surplus to
current requirements of that kind.

It can be stated that the pressure groups, with
no legacies as yet, do not depend upon them! It can
also be said that, on financial showing alone, they,
with CCE, MHA and RADAR seem to be in the most
healthy condition, though CHAR was at pains to say
this was so only as the result of cuts in staff in
1980/81. RADAR referred to 'careful housekeeping
allowing the association to build up a comfortable
reserve which is vital', and to the assumption that
'legacies will enable to association to build up
essential funds to provide a sound financial basis
for its work in the future': the fund raising
department had increased net income by 10%. 'All
voluntary organisations face a problem of equating
expenditure to income', wrote RADAR, but seemed to
be achieving this more satisfactorily than most.

Although getting government grants WEA still
found itself in financial difficulties. Expenditure
had exceeded income in the past two years despite
reductions in staff. It is perhaps significant that
its income both from investments and legacies was
very small, and it seems that central fund-raising
has played little part in the past, though there has

been extensive fund-raising locally.

Voluntary organisations have to cut their coats according to their cloth, except housing associations which are deliberately left by the government in the ulcer-producing situation of running at a deficit and applying each year for it to be met by government funds. Apart from the latter, there is generally some risk-taking, either by expenditure which assumes that someone will die and leave enough to meet it, or that the fact of a deficit will encourage donations which would not otherwise have materialised. The accounts tell us something of how well the organisations have been playing this game, but they do not tell us whether income and expenditure could both have been greater if there had been more efforts and perhaps more risk-taking. Impressions about this have to be obtained in other ways, and the possibilities and probabilities of voluntary organisations playing a larger part in the future will be described in our final chapter. Next, however, we will look at that most crucial resource, the committee which governs the organisation.

REFERENCES

1. Stevenson, Olive. 'The Barclay Committee: Some Reflections'. In Journal of Social Policy, April 1983.
2. Mullin, Redmond. Present Alms. On the conception of philanthropy, (p.22). Phlogiston Publishing, Birmingham, 1980.
3. Voluntary Action, Winter 1981, p.4.
4. Murray, Nicholas. 'It's a totally different job now'. In Community Care, March 3, 1983.
5. Kramer, Ralph M. Voluntary Agencies in the Welfare State. (p.109) University of California Press, London, 1981.
6. Streatfield D. and Wilson T. The vital link: information in Social Services Departments. Joint Unit for Social Services Research, Sheffield University, 1980.
7. Op. cit. p.33.
8. Hall, Land, Parker and Webb. Change, Choice and Conflict in Social Policy. (p.504). Heinemann Educational Books, London, 1975.
9. Younghusband, E. Social Work in Britain: 1950 - 1975. George Allen and Unwin, London 1978.
10. Op. cit. p.148.

Chapter 4

COMMITTEES

> Directorship is more serious, more responsible,
> more critically important than a short sharp
> trot through a bundle of monthly papers.
>
> - On the Board. (Geoffrey Mills)

Much of the criticism directed at voluntary
organisations recently has been on the ways their
governing bodies are recruited. Murray commented
that 'The electoral process, though right and
proper, is somewhat ineffective as a general method
of change in a voluntary organisation'. (1) Johnson
had doubts about allocating voluntary social
services a more important role because of a number
of features which included 'questionable internal
democracy and a middle-class bias in the recruitment
of members and voluntary workers'. (2) The Housing
Corporation has urged housing associations to 'widen
the basis of membership which elects their
management committees', (3) seeing a danger that
these committees might become self-perpetuating
oligarchies: though Noble pointed out that even
with a large membership there may be 'little exchange
between the membership and their management
committees'. (4)
    Comments have also been made on the composition
of the committees that run voluntary organisations,
however elected or selected:

> First, what is commonly seen on charity boards?
> Most conspicuously, lists of more or less well-
> known names, or the wives and husbands of
> famous names. These recur on large numbers of
> lists; it is clear that they are there simply
> as testimonials to the probity of the charity.
> They have probably accepted the invitation
> reciprocally from friends already on the board;
> the re-cycling and circulation of patrons and
> board members are easily observed phenomena.
> (5)

Mullin's asperity has been matched by Mills who,

referring to companies in a wider context, urged
them not to appoint 'civil servants (retired),
admirals (retired), lords, MPs, big names who are
happy to passively make weight. Nor chums'.(6)
Mullin adds more positively that:

> The criteria should rather be a knowledge of
> the field and a committed interest in it,
> specialised skills (legal, financial, academic,
> managerial, practical) relevant to the needs
> and the organisation's programmes, the time and
> inclination to attend meetings and to
> understand the existing and emergent issues, a
> disinterested outlook which gives primacy to
> the needs not to the board's tranquillity or
> dignity or to a merely emotional resistance to
> change. (7)

In the light of these comments we must now
examine how the governing bodies of our sample are
theoretically and in practice recruited and what
their composition turns out to be. Throughout the
chapter they will now be referred to collectively as
'committees', though when reference is made to
individual organisations the appropriate terms may
be different.

The committees varied considerably in size from
MHA at 10, to RADAR at 40 and WEA 42. Nine
organisations had 11 - 28 and the median is 19. At
this point and at others in this chapter, some
interesting comparisons may be made with Kramer's
study of organisations for the handicapped: in
Britain Kramer (8) found a range of 10 - 120 with a
mean size of 23.

THE RECRUITMENT OF COMMITTEES

More than half of the sample (10) were constituted
as companies; of the others, five were charitable
associations and three housing associations. All
the companies and housing associations have annual
elections, and members of the committees are elected
for three years: this applied also to one of the
charitable associations, so 14 in all operated on
this basis. Of the other four, three had an annual,
and one a triennial election of the whole committee.

On paper therefore, democratic election
processes prevail. Enquiries revealed, however,
that only a few organisations experience much
competition for places, and in most cases the
committee itself nominates members to fill vacancies

and - there being no competition - no election is necessary. Membership is reviewed regularly or occasionally by the chairman, often after discussion with the CEO and others, and proposals are made to the committee. Chairmen mostly reported no difficulty in finding suitable people to serve, though in certain cases where their requirements were rigorous - that people should have specific and relevant qualifications, and/or should be able to give large amounts of time to the work - it was mentioned that it was a lengthy process.

If we ask whether the committees' composition clearly results from active participation of a wide section of the organisation's membership we could answer affirmatively only in the case of six. These are BDA, CHAR, FNF, NAWCH, NGEC and WEA, - a 'democratic elect'. In two of these organisations, FNF and NGEC, there was active participation of a wide section of the membership simply because it was small and individual and met on a face-to-face basis to appoint the committee. Both organisations are relatively young, single-cause, bodies with a substantial number of members being personally affected by the issues with which the organisations are concerned.

In the other four bodies significant numbers of committee members were appointed through branch or equivalent representation. Thus, of the 22 members of the Executive Council of the BDA, 15 are elected by the branches in six separate voting areas, the remaining members being nominated or appointed by the Council itself. The branches' representatives meet in Regional Councils and at the rallies organised by those Councils, and this presumably helps to make candidates for the Executive Council places known to those who have to elect representatives.

Similarly, seven of the seventeen members of the Executive Committee of NAWCH came from the 60 or so branches; and in the WEA 21 members are District Representatives, 2 represent District Secretaries, 2 represent tutor organisers, and 6 trade unions, a total of 31 out of 42.

Of the 14 members of the Executive Committee of CHAR all but 2 are elected by non-statutory member organisations and 11 Regional Groups, and the process seems to be a lively one, which had made a complete change of committee membership, officers excepted, in three years! This is not strictly branch representation, but the constituent bodies got plenty of opportunity to meet people from other

organisations and groups in the general meetings of
the membership which are called three times a year
in different parts of the country, are well
attended, and have a real say in the work of the
campaign.

These four organisations are therefore
different in that their constitutions compel their
committees to be subject to changes made by a wider
membership, though we cannot assume that because
branches or groups send representatives to the
national committee these representatives result from
a process in which the membership generally takes an
active and interested part. It could be that there
is a process of 'scraping the barrel' locally to
find someone willing and able to go, with no
competition for the place and no election. The
greater apparent democracy in these organisations
could be rather hollow. Unfortunately the study
could not extend to an examination of the
functioning of local bodies, so no clear answers to
this can be given, though the impression received at
the centre was that local democratic procedures were
meaningful.

Of the other twelve organisations seen, one
(MHCAA) is excluded from this discussion as its new
memorandum and articles following the merger of two
bodies had just come into effect and there was no
experience to describe; the other eleven all
generally have uncontested elections of their
committees at Annual Meetings, the candidates being
nominated by the committee itself and being of the
exact number to fill the places available. This is
the situation which it seems is deplored by the
Housing Corporation in the reports it makes on the
monitoring of housing associations' work: in one
report, for example, its comment was that '.....
membership of the Association at the time of the
monitoring visit stood at 29. This number is not
sufficient to enable the Committee to be
democratically accountable or to provide a pool of
talent from which new Committee members can be
drawn. A broader membership base is recommended for
such a large nationally based association.' (The
committee membership at the time numbered 13).

It is therefore interesting to note the
memberships of the eleven organisations subject to
this criticism of not being 'democratically
accountable'. In four cases membership of the
association and of the committee was identical:
numbers were equal. Of the others, membership
numbers were 38, 50, 100, 160, 500, 1,000, and

2,100. At what point the Housing Corporation would have expected the number to be large enough their report did not say, perhaps not even as high as 100 - but the situation found in this sample surely makes nonsense of their contention. It is not size of membership that makes for contested elections. However broad the membership base, members may not come to Annual Meetings, and may not wish to serve on the committee. It seemed from reports on the eleven organisations that members attending AGMs who were not committee members were relatively small, the possible exceptions to this being JGAD and HCT.

These then are the ways the committees come into being. They point the need for further thinking about what democracy means, or ought to mean, in voluntary organisations: but before we give some attention to this it is important to know something about the committees that presently govern them, how adequate they are, and whether the ways in which they are elected make significant differences to their composition.

THE COMPOSITION OF COMMITTEES

Perhaps the most obvious test of the worth of a committee is the extent to which its members are knowledgeable about the subject(s) with which they have to deal, though this is not to say that a concern for a cause, not necessarily combined with any expert knowledge, is to be spurned, and for this reason one will expect a proportion of members to be 'lay' in the context of the work involved. An examination of the composition of the committees of all the organisations in our sample shows that 13 at least have 50% or more in the expert category, and in two it was certainly less. The remainder comprised BDA, whose committee expertise in the activities undertaken by the Association might be questioned, but nearly all of whom were themselves deaf: CHAR, whose committee is almost wholly composed of professional CHAR workers and 'community activists', experts in the cause but whose wider expertise could not be identified: and WEA, for which the expertise that is relevant is not obvious, unless it be narrowly defined as 'teaching', in which case the composition was low. It would also be true to say that, with these qualifications, committees had a large proportion of business or professional people in their membership, though it might not be as high as Kramer's 'two-thirds to more than three-quarters'.

Class

At this point it is appropriate to comment on
Johnson's criticism of 'middle-class bias' in the
recruitment of members. To what extent is this
criticism justified? We must define the term
'middle class' before we can answer the question.
As to who are the middle classes, The Times in 1975
wrote: 'They can be defined in relatively
restricted terms so that they appear to be a small
minority of senior professional men, or they can be
defined to include everyone who owns his own house,
or works in a white-collar job. In that case the
middle class is at least half our society'.(9) As
Ian Bradley has stated, the latter approach is more
usually accepted:

> Polls in which people are invited to assess
> their own social class position, the social
> classifications derived from the national
> census, and the investigations of market
> researchers, all give remarkably similar
> results. They agree that the middle classes
> are to be defined principally by their
> occupations, that they are made up of broadly
> those who do non-manual jobs and their
> families, and that they form 40 per cent or
> more of the population. (10)

On this definition the very fact that most
committees have 50% or more members with 'expert'
knowledge weights the membership towards the middle
class. Medicine for CHSA, law and social work for
FNF, nursing for NAWCH, education for WEA, to take
but a few examples, give non-manual, indeed
professional, weightings, and are desirable, we have
already suggested, for the quality performance of
the organisations concerned. Add to these the
knowledge of management, accountancy, business from
which all would no doubt benefit, and most do, and
more middle-class 'weight' is inevitable.
    If there are manual workers on committees they
will be there because of other qualities that they
can contribute, and one might expect that perhaps
half of the 'lay' members would fall into the
category: but it is plain from an examination of
the occupations of committee members in our sample
that this is not the case. Three bodies referred to
earlier whose committees do not have experts
predominating are concerned with deafness, homelessness and adult education - all causes with which

manual workers might be expected to be at least as concerned as white-collar workers: yet the BDA committee has at least two thirds in middle-class occupations; the committee of CHAR is, as has been said, largely composed of professional activists for the cause, some of whom may have had 'working-class' roots but by the present definition are certainly non-manual, middle class; and WEA committee members are all but a few in non-manual occupations. Some might say the NGEC is an exception to the middle-class predominance for it has 55% gypsies in its membership; yet at interview, I was told that gypsies are all 'small businessmen', whom some would call middle class!

Johnson's use of the word 'bias' implies that the absence of manual workers on committees is due to middle-class prejudice, i.e. an unwillingness to invite or nominate suitable people who are manual workers for committee membership. I had no evidence of there being such a prejudice, and it is more likely that manual workers are not there because any that would like to serve are not known within the organisation. Some studies have suggested that the 'working classes' are not found in movements of the sort we are examining because they do not wish to be there: Chamberlain, for example, maintained that they extensively believe that 'present political arrangements do not work particularly well, and that it is through direct action and class solidarity that working class people can best make themselves heard'. (11) The following is a reference to Hausknecht which gives a deeper explanation:

> Like Gans and other recent observers of the working class, he sees the blue-collar worker as a member of a distinctive sub-culture. In this culture, life is focused on the family, which also provides the model for all social relationships. These relationships are largely personal or primary and the worker is only minimally committed to the impersonal or secondary relationship of the society beyond the family. He neither understands nor trusts the larger community. His 'misanthropic' and intolerant perception of others, combined with a fatalistic feeling that he is powerless to change the world, result in his avoiding the voluntary association with its impersonal social relationships. (12)

It is not within the scope or capacity of the present author to comment on the validity of these arguments, though many would agree that there is, for whatever reason, less tradition of participation in organisations of the kind we are studying, amongst manual workers. It would have been illuminating if the present study had been able to analyse membership and other support of the sample organisations by class. However, Bradley and others tell us that the middle class is expanding in numbers and the working class shrinking. Perhaps we may reasonably hope that the situation will thus be rectified by events, but in the meantime present members should be considering this matter and examining their motives and attitudes in recruitment of new members.

Consumer Representation

It is certainly important that committee members should be knowledgeable, and what committees do will certainly be of better quality if one-class membership can be avoided. It is perhaps even more important than either of these that there should be intimate understanding of the viewpoint of the 'consumer' of the services which the organisation provides, or with whose policy it is concerned. This may be represented either at committee level, or by systematic research into consumer views, or through an intelligence system which provides regular and balanced 'feedback' from the point of delivery of services.

We have seen from the previous chapter that very little study of consumer views or of 'feedback' is undertaken (NAWCH being a notable exception) so the representation of consumers, whether by election or selection, on committees is that much more important. Kramer found that one-third of the board members were consumers. In our sample, as we have just seen, BDA heads the list with nearly 100%. FNF committee also had a membership almost wholly of people with problems of access to their children following divorce. Six other committees had significant representation of the consumer, and this applied to all but CHAR of the 'democratic elect' referred to on page 86, but ten including CHAR had no representation at all. The 'consumer' in a number of cases was not likely to be a ready committee member - the homeless, the frail elderly, children, for example: in such cases the arguments for having systematic information from the 'coal-

face' and/or members of committee who work with the
relevant client groups are even stronger.

In other cases the comment was that the
consumer 'might be too personally involved', or that
it was 'not permissible', as in the tenants of a
housing association. Though this latter contention
is in fact questionable, for some associations do
have representatives of tenants on their committees,
there is no doubt that there is potential conflict
of interest between tenants and others. A booklet
of the National Federation of Housing Associations
has this to say:

> The long-term objectives of the Association, in
> terms of its future development and in terms of
> the people who will be seeking its
> accommodation in the years ahead, needs to be
> balanced against the more immediate needs of
> the current consumer. Except for mutual
> associations - where tenants and members are
> the same - all associations have obligations in
> perpetuity. The association, particularly if
> it is on charitable Model Rules, must not place
> the desires of existing tenants (e.g. for low
> rents or for the personal ownership of their
> homes) above the needs of future tenants (e.g.
> for high maintenance standards or simply for a
> home to live in). (13)

As the present writer put it elsewhere:

> Add to this the fact that many associations
> have very wide policy considerations to bear in
> mind (such as whether to build in one part of
> the country or another, whether to go in for
> leasehold, what emphasis to give to residential
> qualifications, how to raise funds from non-
> public sources) whereas tenants per se are
> concerned largely with the management aspects
> of their own estates, and it will be seen that
> tenant representation is no straightforward
> matter. (14)

This picture may be mirrored in other contexts,
and the problems faced, but the facts remain that
there is a continuing responsibility on all
voluntary organisations to maximise their knowledge
of the people for whom they are working in all
possible ways, and that it is not clear that all are
doing so.

Staff Representation

Though we have made it clear that this is not a study of management, and participation of staff at all levels in the functioning of the organisation is essentially a management issue, it is appropriate here to make some reference to the question of formal staff representation on committees. (By this is meant the appointment by staff of certain committee members: staff presence on occasions at committee meetings in an advisory role is assumed to be normal). Of the sixteen organisations in the sample employing staff, only one, CA, had such representation, and the others that expressed their views had two main responses to the idea. The first was that it would not be desirable in that the narrower interests of staff per se, and those of the organisation as a whole or the aims it existed to pursue, could sometimes conflict; and the clear implication was that committee members should be elected for the wider role, leaving resolution of any such conflict to be settled either outside the committee or between the committee and the staff in a direct negotiating role.

The second response made by several organisations was that charitable status could be jeopardised by having staff representation on the committee. This issue was raised also by the Church Army, the organisation that set up a Working Party in 1979 'To make recommendations to the Board of ways in which the Memorandum and Articles of the Association could be changed in order to facilitate greater participation by Officers on policy making for the Society'. It has to be explained that 'Officers' in CA meant at that time 'Commissioned Officers' i.e. senior paid members of staff, of whom there were several hundred.

The Working Party's proposals included:-

1. A membership of CA consisting of 'A' Members and 'B' Members, the latter of whom are solely Commissioned Officers.
2. Board membership to be elected by 'A' and 'B' Members at the Annual General Meeting. 'B' Members not to be entitled otherwise to vote at General Meetings.
3. The Board to consist of between twenty and thirty members of whom six would be 'B' members of CA.
4. 'B' Members on the Board entitled to vote on any matter coming before the Board

except one affecting 'the remuneration and conditions and benefits of service and obligations' of Commissioned Officers or Officers of CA (Chief Secretary, Chief Accountant, Honorary Treasurer etc.).

It seemed that the Charity Commission would accept proposals 1 and 2 but might not accept 3 and 4, on the grounds that 'The Commission would certainly not countenance any amendment to the Memorandum and Articles which would place the Officers in a position either as Members of the Governing Body or Members of the Company, where they could influence decisions affecting their own interests as employees of the Company'. (This was despite the fact that the Board operating under the 1892 Articles had 6 Officers in its membership, appointed directly by the Board). In a separate paper the Charity Commission made it clear that it saw placing the Officers in such a position as on a par with enabling trustees of charities to benefit from charitable funds, which would be 'incompatible with the concept of charity'.

It is interesting to note in passing that at least one housing association, as reported by the NFHA, has reserved places on the Committee for staff representatives, elected for a one-year period and not eligible for re-election: 'this means', the Federation comments, 'that, over a period of time, a growing number of staff get to know the workings of the Committee from the inside and have a deeper appreciation - while being able to make a full contribution - of their associations' work'. (15)

Sex

All but three of the organisations have substantially more men than women on their management committees, indeed 12 out of 18 had over 70% men. This compares with Kramer who found that women comprised 'about one-third' of all board members. The three with a female predominance were JGAD, FEGH and NAWCH: the men and women on FEGH nevertheless indicated their clear ideas about the different roles of the sexes by having a Finance Committee of 9 men, and a Case Committee and a Homes Committee each of 12 women. NAWCH commented at interview on their regret at having only one man on their committee of 22.

Reasons could be ascribed for the apparent continued old-fashionedness of attitudes which gives

pride of place to men as committee members. As we
have seen, most organisations seek a selection of
people who have relevant professional qualifications
for their committee work, and the fact that of those
active in many professions - particularly at the
stage of life when they can take time to offer to
voluntary work - men predominate, must tip the
scales considerably. An organisation like Families
Need Fathers might reasonably expect to have father-
predominance though it manages to have 3 women
members on its 20-member committee. The MHCAA
commented without prompting on their shortage of
women, adding almost in the same breath that one
barrier to getting new members is Clause 4 of their
Memorandum of Association which requires total
allegiance to an Evangelical interpretation of
Christianity including 'The whole Bible as the
inspired Word of God', and it seemed possible that
this made it easier to get parsons than lay women.
    Despite these qualifications however, the
overall impression remains, of a certain old-
fashionedness. Disability, old age and housing are
subjects of equal if not greater significance for
women as for men: so it might be expected that
numbers of each would be roughly equal on the
committees of RADAR, CCE and HCT. Much the same
might be said of BDA, Church Army and WEA. Yet men
predominate.
    Those who go the other way however are also
open to criticism. The subcommittee composition of
FEGH shows a certain Victorianism, and the main
committee of NAWCH is little better in that it
implies that only women are suitable to consider the
welfare of children.
    Committee members are of a fascinating variety:
from the young activists of CHAR, to the genteel and
upper class FEGH; from the predominance of parsons
in MHCAA to that of gypsies in NGEC; from the
eminent medicos of CHSA to the motherly social
workers and nurses of NAWCH. There is very little
trace of what Redmond Mullin saw on 'charity
boards', - the large numbers of 'more or less well-
known names'. On the whole all are impressive as
groups of people able to do a good job in the
context of their particular organisation. They need
to consider whether they are unduly one-class, or
one-sex, or lacking in those who belong to or
closely understand the relevant client-groups, or
should have staff representation: but let it be
firmly added that 'token' representation of any
sector may be worse than no representation at all.

To choose someone as a committee member because he
is a manual worker or she is a woman, without their
having primarily some other particular quality to
bring to the committee's deliberations, is insulting
because it is patronising and can do no one any
good. Similar considerations apply to consumer or
staff representation, with the addition that
consumers or staff selected or elected as such
should be people reasonably able to sound out the
views of others and so have some authority in
speaking for them.

MEMBERSHIP CHANGE AND ATTENDANCE

These comments are all based on the situations
prevailing at the time of interview and were drawn
from a consideration of the quality of the
membership of the committees. There are two other
aspects which may shed light on the effectiveness of
these committees - the degree of change of
membership, and the adequacy of attendance at
meetings. On the former, it is important that there
should be change, to give the stimulus of 'new
blood', but not so much of it that a continuity of
thought and policy is jeopardized. The chairman of
one organisation, BDA, indicated that he thought
there was too little change, and BDA had 3 - 4 new
members out of 20 each triennium, an average of 6%
per annum. If we take a criterion of less than 10%
average change per annum, three others fell into
this category, Church Army, FEGH and John Grooms.
FNF reported too much change, and if this is taken
to be 33.3% per annum, CHAR and NAWCH will go with
it. Two organisations (MHCAA and RADAR) had
recently changed their constitutions so are not
included in this particular analysis (Church Army
were also in the process of doing so but are
included), so there are 9 bodies out of 16 whose
degree of change could be said to be moderate. On
this matter Kramer found a 'policy of re-electing
the board members and not replacing more than 10%
each year'.
What then of the attendance at committee
meetings? This is summarised in Table 4.1.

Table 4.1:   Attendance at Committee Meetings

Number of committee meetings per annum	No. of organisations by average attendance at committee meetings			
	less than 50%	50%-	75%-	90% and over
4	–	4	3	2
5	–	1	–	–
6	–	–	–	1
8 or more	–	3	2	–

N = 16

All the organisations in the sample reported more than 50% attendance, half of them in the 50% but under 75% range, and the others more than that. The committees of the two single-cause personal-membership organisations, FNF and NGEC, meeting every 5 weeks and 10 weeks respectively, are in the 50% to 75% attendance range, as is CHAR, meeting 8 times per annum. NAWCH is one in the 75% – 90% range, and BDA and WEA indicated 90% or more; all three meet quarterly. Kramer's comment on attendance was that 'In England, where rates of attendance of 75 to 90 per cent was reported, only seven out of the twenty boards meet monthly; another four were convened bimonthly and the remaining nine only three or four times a year'.

There are two matters which may affect attendances at committee meetings on which it would have been good to have had more information. One is the times at which meetings take place: FEGH, for example, find that their Case Committee, due to the professional social workers on it, like to meet in the mornings; its Homes Committee, with a considerable number of housewives involved, in the afternoons; and its Finance Committee at 4.30 p.m. The other matter is the cost of attendance: a national organisation may deter representatives from far afield if they, or their branches, have to find the fares: if expenses are paid from central funds the picture may be different. As a compromise however, as WEA have found, a pooling of fares scheme may improve attendance.

It may be concluded from this examination of the composition of committees that in many respects the extent to which committee members are there as result of a membership actively electing them has little effect on quality or functioning. Attendances at meetings seem much the same; organisations with a wide 'personal' electorate seem perhaps to produce committees stronger in their representation of consumers, but weaker in relevant expertise; and they tend to produce too much change of committee membership - as the chairmen see it - though BDA is a notable exception. None of these are matters which point overwhelmingly to a need for constitutional reform, for they could be altered within the systems now prevailing. We have reached the point at which we need to discuss the issues of 'democracy', in the context of the management of voluntary organisations, at a more fundamental level.

DEMOCRACY

There has recently been much talk loosely about 'democracy and accountability'. These two features are often lumped together, as if they were the same thing, generally without more precision or definition. Thus, for example, in October 1982, the Housing Associations Branch of NALGO 'called for greater democracy and accountability within the voluntary housing movement', which presumably, in its view, did not measure up to local government or trade union practices in this respect. In this chapter we are concerned only with democracy, though its links with accountability will become evident and we shall go on to consider the latter in a subsequent chapter.

Democracy is defined in the Concise Oxford Dictionary as 'government by the people, direct or representative'. 'Government' in this definition means the body of persons governing a state, 'the people' being all the citizens of that state, and when applied to voluntary organisations 'the people' can only mean the members of the organisation, though one wonders sometimes whether NALGO and similar critics want all voluntary organisations to be governed by 'the people' in the widest sense, - nominees presumably of a body elected by 'the people' such as a local authority. One has only to state this to see how impracticable, let alone undesirable, this is. The sheer numbers of nominees involved makes it impracticable: and even if people could be found, what sort of democracy is government by local authority nominees?

Where would the line be drawn? - are all voluntary organisations to be included? - the football club, the Women's Institute? We must assume that this is not what the critics have in mind, but rather that they are demanding that voluntary organisations improve their processes of internal democracy.

As we have seen, membership of voluntary bodies may number anything from a very few to many thousands. They have joined because they want to do or to advocate something, or to give of their knowledge or expertise in what seems to be a good cause. As Robson wrote: 'Compassion still exists to compel effective action .... There is a vast amount of both voluntary and vocational work being carried out for a multitude of different causes by men and women whose chief motive is compassion'. (16). The majority of those governing the organisations covered by this study were undoubtedly motivated by compassion or a wider social concern, though certainly qualified occasionally by some personal need. In a neat phrase ascribed to Francis Gladstone, 'A voluntary organisation exists because it may and not because it must'. People have freedom to associate and how they govern their affairs is their own responsibility. No one has the right to tell them what democratic procedures to adopt, though if they wish to have a corporate entity at law they will have to adopt certain rules and abide by them. No one can dictate what their aims are to be, though if they wish to have certain privileges, such as charitable status, they will have to tailor their aims accordingly: if they appeal for funds, or employ staff, or own property, other obligations will arise, and they must conform like the rest of us to the law: but the law does not lay down what democracy is in voluntary organisations, and then insist upon it; no one has the right to insist on new members being admitted to an association, simply to make it superficially more democratic.

It may be noted in passing that there are thousands of charitable trusts in the field of social welfare for which no democratic practices apply at all. Trustees have been appointed to carry out certain functions with funds provided by endowments, and will appoint additional trustees as and when they think fit. It is curious that there are no vociferous requests that they should be democratised, whereas when some degree of democracy is written into the rules of an association more is asked for by critics from outside. Some voluntary

organisations are midway between charitable trusts
and the free democratic association of individual
members: in our sample, the RBLHA was established
to provide a housing arm for the Royal British
Legion, to benefit the same category of persons viz.
ex-servicemen, and whilst such persons exist it
would be unreasonable to expect the housing association to do another job or be governed by a wider
group of people than those from the Legion itself,
as is the case. Or to take another example, from
outside our sample, the Centre for Policy on Ageing;
it was started by the Nuffield Foundation to carry
out one of the purposes laid down by the founder,
Lord Nuffield, viz. 'the care and comfort of the
aged poor'; the Foundation therefore nominates 4 of
the 8 members of the Board of Governors. There is
little democracy there, for even the additional 4 -
6 members of the Board depend upon nomination by the
Board itself.

'Government by the people, direct or representative'. The organisations in our sample will all,
no doubt, wish to feel that 'the people', their
members, have the ultimate say in how the
association conducts it affairs. For those face-to-
face organisations, FNF and NGEC there seems little
doubt that this is so. For the four organisations
with branch or similar election procedures we have
seen that it seems likely that something approaching
full marks for democracy may be allotted. What of
the remainder, whose constitutions lay down how
committees shall be elected, i.e. how representative
democracy shall work, but which find that it is
honoured - so far as elections are concerned - only
in the letter? Is democracy failing? Does the
situation imply that the organisation is governed by
a clique, failing in vigour, out of touch with the
membership, possibly astray even on policies proper
to the aims of the organisation? There is no
evidence that it implies any of these things.

In the first place it is in the nature of many
organisations in these fields that they are 'joined'
by people who wish to support the cause they
represent, the work they do, but who do not wish to
participate in the government of the organisation in
any way. They are sleeping partners, happy to be so
because they are satisfied with the aims of the
organisation and the methods it is adopting to
achieve them. Which of my readers does not belong
to several organisations, or subscribe to them, in
this sort of way? A well written Annual Report will
often be adequate to retain their support. A few

may also attend the Annual General Meeting: but the
fact that they do not put up candidates for election
to the committee does not imply that the
organisation is moribund, only that the membership
of the organisation is satisfied with the committee
it has.   It implies that the committee itself is
keeping to the aims of the organisation and, because
its members are themselves committed to them and
perhaps because they have grass-roots contacts with
the wider membership, are acting in the ways their
supporters approve.   If members are not resigning,
or subscriptions falling off, if there is no uproar
in the AGM, the committee may feel that it has the
support that it should have.   In this respect they
are in much the same position as the Board of a
business company, whose indicators are the standing
of its shares on the stock market and in extremis
the strength of any feeling expressed in the General
Meeting: though the parallel is not exact, the
charitable company or association does not compare
unfavourably with the commercial world.   As the
Institute of Directors has written:

> .... the hard fact remains that it is only in
> times of trouble that shareholders appear to
> take any active interest in the company's
> affairs; not one per cent will attend a company
> meeting, very few ever read a company report or
> progress statement, and not many will even
> complete a proxy form unless specially asked to
> do so and given the return postage.   In view of
> the widespread differences in the financial and
> business acumen of shareholders, this is hardly
> surprising. (17)

Is this comfortable defence of the status quo
all that needs to be said?   Are those who complain
of lack of democracy totally wide of the mark?   Is
there no foundation for their criticisms?   In my
view the answer is certainly 'no' to all these
questions.   There are undoubtedly a number of
weaknesses which ought to be faced.   I do not think
that the critics are all dogmatists insisting on
adherence to a theoretical concept of representative
democracy in every context.   Some may be at heart
not really in favour of non-statutory organisations
at all, and using the non-democracy argument as a
convenient stick to beat them with.   In the main
however I believe the critics are asking implicitly,
whether or not they have formulated them in a
positive way, that certain criteria should be

applied to the structure and practices of committees of voluntary organisations. I would myself formulate them as follows:

The Committee should

1. adequately represent the membership in what it does
2. have amongst its membership a range of knowledge or expertise to enable it to do its work convincingly and effectively
3. be refreshed regularly with new ideas and/or new blood
4. be un-sentimental in purging itself of chronic non-attenders
5. subject itself to the scrutiny of its membership at least annually or on demand, as a safety valve in time of crisis.

It may now be valuable to enlarge on certain of these and consider the ways in which voluntary organisations could be meeting them; and in doing so we may remember that 'voluntary organisations' in the scope of this study includes charitable trusts, and that criteria 2, 3 and 4 may equally be applied to them.

Criterion No.1. Adequately represent the members. We have already discussed a number of aspects of this, and concluded that it is not simply a matter of there being democratic mechanisms or whether these are vigorously used. We have seen that where there are branches there may be better chances of involving the membership in the choice of committee, though the committees found in other organisations do not appear to differ greatly in quality or functioning. It is to be noted that RADAR is giving attention to this matter. Its Annual Report for 1980-81 reads:

During the year Regional Conferences have been held at Bath, Bristol, Chorley, Keswick, Leeds, Northampton, Wolverhampton and Worcester ... A regional system is slowly evolving by which it is hoped that more regional meetings can be held to allow for greater discussion of local topics and issues. The forthcoming appoint- ments of additional development officers to work in the North and South-West will allow this process to develop more rapidly.

It is worth considering whether there is scope for other organisations to build into their constitutions places on their committees to be filled by representatives of branches or groups of people who, because of geographical or occupational factors know one another reasonably well. The suggestion would pose enormous questions if taken seriously. Stonham Housing Association is moving in that direction: it is proposing to co-opt committee members from each region, and eventually may have Regional Councils whose chairmen will be members of the council of management of the Association. When there are significant local topics to be discussed at local level, as the references in the RADAR Annual Report quoted above imply, a regional organisation may be relevant and perhaps in the case of SHA some devolution of responsibilities would be possible, though far from easy. In both these cases, the basis for election of representatives to the committee might be readily established: but what of other bodies in our sample? What are the local activities, on which branch or regional organisation would surely have to be based?
    Table 4.2 summarises the situation:

Table 4.2: Local activities in organisations with no branch representation

Organisation	Local Activity
CHSA	Branches in Scotland and Northern Ireland. 38 volunteer stroke schemes, 202 affiliated stroke clubs.
CA	25 residential establishments and other concerns
CCE	None
FEGH	11 residential homes for the elderly
HCT	3 branches
JGAD	6 areas with residential establishments 6 - 7 local fund raising groups
MHCAA	several residential homes all in Croydon
MHA	9 country houses, each with informal house committees
RBLHA	About 250 housing schemes, each with a house committee
Sh.H & A	8 establishments of which 5 are in London

It will be seen that none of those listed has a network of branches or affiliated groups of the sort found in the bodies already discussed. Those that do have branches of any sort have two or three. Some organisations have 'house committees' attached to housing schemes, on which 'branch' or 'regional' representation might be built, and CHSA has volunteer groups and clubs which might be similarly used, but mostly the organisations are running services which are essentially directed from a head office, and there does not seem much likelihood of building a local group structure except on something quite new. This would be creating a new organisation simply to make the election of the committee 'more democratic'. Though it is right that all organisations should consider the matter in the context of their own circumstances, this does not seem a very likely general development to be recommended.

It has also to be recognised that the problems of getting a committee adequately representative of a very large membership are very great, however democratic the elections and other processes in theory are, and however vigorously they are used. This was amply demonstrated by the National Trust in 1982, when the Trust's leasing of land to the RAF for building a 'bunker' headquarters brought considerably controversy. The Trust has 1,100,000 members, who elect half the members of the Council, the other half being appointed by certain societies and organisations relevant to the work of the Trust. Voting is by proxy and the problem is not in getting nominees to contest places, but that there is little chance of an 'outsider', not standing for re-election or nominated by the Council or members of the Council, becoming well enough known to attract enough support to gain a place. There are Regional Committees, ostensibly making opportunities for some to become known to fellow-members, but there are 14 of these committees so opportunities are not wide-spread, and they do not elect members to the Council – quite the reverse, the Regional Committees are appointed by the Executive Committee, itself elected by the Council. The scope for 'in-breeding' is therefore large, however well-intentioned the Council and Executive Committee are.

The use of proxy voting too is unsatisfactory, in that it means that even if members attend General Meetings in person and have useful debate it will have little effect on voting, because vastly greater numbers of proxy votes have been cast beforehand and cannot be affected, nor indeed can any resolution be amended for a similar reason - that proxy voters have not had a chance to vote on it. At the Extraordinary General Meeting of the Trust called to discuss the 'bunker' there were 2,500 members present - even that making real debate difficult because of the numbers - and including proxies there were 196,543 votes. Yet even on that controversial issue votes represented only 18% of the membership. The resolution was lost, though amongst those actually present at the General Meeting there was a majority for it. Yet no one could sensibly argue that the Trust should be governed by the votes only of that small proportion of the membership, 4% on this occasion, who could get to the meeting in person. There is no adequate answer but that the committees of organisations of this size must make continuous and conscious efforts to keep themselves in touch with the membership: the National Trust seemingly <u>could</u> improve its constitutional arrangements by having members elected by the Regions, but that may not be so in other organisations and as we have seen this is not the only, or necessarily an adequate, answer in itself. Fortunately, one might say, there are not many bodies in the fields covered by the current study that have so acute a problem of size.

To represent the membership adequately is an aim which cannot be achieved in many organisations solely by constitutional arrangements, though these must be closely attended to, but by a variety of deliberate efforts on the part of members of the Committee, individually and corporately. These may include personal attention to certain aspects of the work and discussions of them with members concerned with them; special gatherings in different parts of the country, of the sort arranged by BDA and CHAR; full and frank Annual Reports made widely available, and careful attention to 'feed-back' on these or any other publications or statements of policy.

<u>Criterion No. 2. Have adequate expertise</u>. We have seen that most committees show up well on this. If anything those with a representation of branches have a lower input of relevant expertise. The WEA makes a modest gesture towards a built-in election of particular expertise, in having two representatives of tutor organisers on the committee. It also has six trade union representatives, which must add some specialties to its counsels, though their relevance is not obvious. Otherwise however our

sample did not produce examples of election on a basis of expertise, and it is likely that in general it is a rare method.

It is therefore important that the committee itself should be constantly on watch for expertise that it lacks, and people who could supply it: often this is something that falls to the chairman in particular, for he is perhaps best placed to identify the needs and, with the help of the CEO, to come across people who might be nominated for committee membership.

This is a matter on which charitable trusts are even more vulnerable than associations, for trusts have no impulse to change or add to their membership unless that impulse comes from within the trustees.

It is relevant here to note the results of a survey of people undertaking voluntary work which was conducted for the Volunteer Centre in 1981.(18) It was found that the two major reasons for interest/involvement in the work were an approach from a friend/neighbour/acquaintance and/or the work itself being part of, or connected with, the main personal interest or skill of the volunteer.

Criterion No.3. Get new ideas and/or new blood. If 'new blood' can be assumed to bring refreshment to a committee's ideas, most of our sample organisations were - as we have seen - reasonably well refreshed, by choice of electorate or as a result of 'natural wastage' making replacements necessary. Only one thought there was not enough change and that was one with branch representation. Again, though, much must rest with the chairman and those he consults, to ensure that the new people brought in are likely to provide fresh thinking. In the case of the charitable trust, where there may be no specifica-tion of a minimum number of trustees, the lack of careful attention to replacements is especially important. A charity by which I was once employed was asked by the Treasury Solicitor to take over a charitable trust all of whose trustees had died some years previously without steps being taken to replace them!

In the case of organisations whose membership is elected a valuable further safeguard in the interest of new blood may lie in a constitutional bar to continued election of existing members e.g. by ineligibility for re-election after 6 years service until a further year has elapsed. This provides the opportunity for others to come in and make their marks without embarrassment. In our sample, however, only one organisation (NAWCH) had a clause to this effect. Despite the fact that three of the other organisations had only recently re-modelled their rules, no modification on these lines had been introduced. It has to be recognised that there is 'vested interest' in not having a compulsory retirement rule: for many, membership of certain voluntary organisation committees is a much-prized thing, and likewise the committees themselves may be loth to lose certain long-established members, even for a year. On the other hand a 'pause for reflection' on the part of all, as well as the deliberate introduction of a new member, is no bad thing. It is also possible that some people whose contribution to the work of a committee would be much valued will agree to join it much more readily if they know what their period of service will be: one of the most effective committees with which I have been connected appointed members for five years, after which period no re-appointment was ever made.

It is possible to introduce new ideas in other ways than by changing committee membership. Some organisations have advisory councils, whose composition may be different from that of the executive committee: if these councils are seriously used, if it is clear that the executive respects their advice, if they are even encouraged further by some executive functions, they can have a vigorous and stimulating part to play. Other organisations have an elected council from which the executive committee is drawn, and if the work is distributed in such a way that the two react upon each other, again stimulation may result. The principle is that of a bicameral constitution, which is admittedly more complicated to administer, and can have its own problems, particularly if there is friction between the two parts, but in the interest of new ideas being generated has much to be said for it.

Criterion No. 4. Purge non-attenders. Our sample showed up quite well on this, in that attendance levels at committee meetings were high. It may not always be so. It has been my own experience to establish a charitable trust in a northern town with 10 local worthies, yet to be told after only 4 or 5 years that it was failing to get a quorum at its meetings. A housing association of my acquaintance set up some subcommittees, with membership selected for their special expertise, but had to re-structure

them after 2 or 3 years because interest was waning.
I am at the moment of writing a member of a
committee composed entirely of two representatives
from each of 7 different geographical areas: two
area representatives did not attend any of the five
meetings in 1982, and one attended only one.

Committees must not be sentimental about this
sort of thing. If a member has had a long illness,
or been prevented for similar good reasons from
attending, allowance must no doubt be made, but
otherwise here is another function for the watchful
chairman, to make pointed enquiries as opportunity
arises, and if necessary to advise a failing member
either to resign or to seek leave of absence if this
is appropriate, so that the committee knows where it
stands. Continuity of attendance is vital to a
committee being effective. The committee should
also remember this when recruiting new members.

<u>Criterion No. 5. Submit policies to the membership.</u>
One of the organisations in the sample (JGAD) is
deliberately extending its membership to people
whose knowledge and interest will, it is hoped,
provide intelligent commentary on what the committee
has done in the year when it reports to the AGM. It
is to be hoped that this is successful, though we
have seen that the experience of most of the others
is not encouraging. Nevertheless it is important
that organisations should prepare careful reports
and accounts and give the membership <u>the chance</u> to
comment: without this there is no 'safety valve'.
Even where, as in the National Trust, an upsurge of
feeling in a crisis can have no direct constitutional effect, the opportunity for dissidents to
address committees is valuable, and - again as in
the National Trust - will be taken account of by any
committee worth its salt.

Committees must account to their members; this
is an essential criterion of democracy. They must
also be responsive to the views of other categories
of persons or organisations to whom they have
obligations. These may be subscribers or trusts or
central or local government departments from which
they obtain funds: they may be the people whose
needs they seek to meet, whether by services
provided or as tenants or residents in properties
owned by the organisations: they may be the
communities within which their activities are set;
they may be the staff they employ. These are
aspects which in my definition are covered by the
word 'accountability', which is often loosely

associated with 'democracy'. We have discussed the
latter in this chapter. We shall not be well placed
to discuss the former until we have seen in more
detail what are the obligations which voluntary
bodies in our particular field enter into in
carrying out their work. 'Accountability' will
therefore be examined in a later chapter.

REFERENCES

1. Murray, G.J. Voluntary Organisations and
   Social Welfare. An administrator's
   impression, (p.24). Oliver and Boyd,
   Edinburgh, 1969.
2. Johnson, Norman. Voluntary Social Services,
   (p.143). Basil Blackwell and Martin
   Robertson, Oxford, 1981.
3. Housing Corporation. In the Public Eye. 1980.
4. Noble, David. 'Committee System', article in
   Roof. January, 1980.
5. Mullin, Redmond. Present Alms. On the
   corruption of Philanthropy, (p.21).
   Phlogiston Publishing, Birmingham, 1980.
6. Mills, Geoffrey. On the Board, (p.199).
   Gower, London, 1981.
7. Op.cit. (p.16).
8. Kramer, Ralph M. Voluntary Agencies in the
   Welfare State. University of California
   Press, London, 1981.
9. The Times. 11th January, 1975.
10. Bradley, Ian. The English Middle Classes,
    (p.24). Collins, London, 1982.
11. Chamberlain, C.W. 'Attitudes towards Direct
    Political Action in Britain', in British
    Political Sociology Yearbook. Volume 3,
    1977.
12. Smith, Constance and Freedman, Anne, Voluntary
    Associations, (p.156). Harvard University
    Press, Cambridge, Massachusetts, 1972. The
    reference is to Hausknecht, Murray, 'The
    Blue-Collar Joiners', in Arthur B. Shostak
    and William Gomberg, eds., Blue-Collar
    World: Prentice-Hall, Englewood Cliffs,
    New Jersey, 1964.
13. National Federation of Housing Associations.
    Membership of Housing Associations and
    their Committees. 1981.
14. Mellor, Hugh. 'Democracy and Accountability in
    Housing Associations' in Housing Review
    May-June 1983.

15. NFHA: op.cit.
16. Robson, W.A. <u>Welfare</u> State <u>and</u> <u>Welfare</u>
      <u>Society.</u> George Allen and Unwin, London
      1976.
17. Institute of Directors. <u>Guidelines</u> <u>for</u>
      <u>Directors</u>, (p.33). 1973.
18. Humble, S. <u>Voluntary</u> Action <u>in</u> <u>the</u> <u>1980s.</u> The
      Volunteer Centre, 1982.

Chapter 5

PARTNERS OR RIVALS

Charities enjoy many privileges, not least the
fiscal and rate reliefs, in return for the
benefit they bring to the community. These
privileges seem to us to carry responsibilities, one of which is that they seek to co-
operate with one another when this is advantag-
eous and when to do otherwise would fail to
deploy charitable resources effectively.

- Charity Law and Voluntary Organisations
(Goodman Committee 1976)

The voluntary social services are good examples
of pressure groups which maintain a low
political profile; but their ability to apply
pressure is real. In part their very existence
can be a political pressure because they
operate as an alternative to government
provision and as a source of comparison for the
critics of government action or inaction.

- Change, Choice and Conflict in Social Policy
(Hall, Land, Parker and Webb. 1978)

It is now getting on for forty years since the
Relieving Officer was the main entree to the
statutory health and social services of the day. He
was well-known in his locality, by his role and as a
person, and was often well-respected, but with the
advent of the modern welfare state he was inevitably
replaced by a number of different authorities, often
known not as people or even by name, but simply as
'the Welfare'. Most men-in-the-street did not know
the social and legislative background which would
have enabled them to be more specific in their
concepts of 'the Welfare', and could not be expected
to do so. Today, after various additional developments, the situation is the same; how many appreciate the differences even between Social Services
Departments and the DHSS? Or know what department
employs a Health Visitor?
The average citizen, let alone the average
client before 1939, must have been even more unsure
of what organisations voluntary social workers came
from. Phyllis Bottome's charming description of an
interview with one of these which took place in an

East London home in 1939 could no doubt have been applied at any time in the previous seventy years:

> The visitor smelt like a flower shop and looked like a large golden fruit upon a kitchen plate. She sat in the best chair that had four legs, and quite a lot of seat. Ben gathered that his mother did not consider this delectable being wholly in the light of an enemy. There was no hostility in the way Mrs. Barton leaned against the table, rather than sat down in the presence of so much dignified luxury. He saw that his mother felt uneasy, but only because she did not want to do what the lady suggested should be done; and yet didn't like saying that she wouldn't do it.(1)

In the case of charities, it was 'the Lady' who came to help, in ways quite different from the Relieving Officer or 'the Welfare'. When the Lady left, the account concludes,

> "Well there," said Mrs. Barton with astonished pride, "That was a Lady, Ben - an' no mistake! It might 'ave been the Queen 'erself from the clothes on 'er; but bless you - it's wot I always tells yer father - they don't mean no 'arm by it!"

Today charities - most of them - have moved on. Like their statutory counterparts they employ specialists, with different attitudes. The fact remains however, that these people are equally anonymous, their origins equally mysterious, to the average client, who knows no difference between Age Concern and Help the Aged, or between MIND and MENCAP. The conclusion we must draw from this is that organisations in the field, offering services to individuals, are regarded in the main not as competitors - like Sainsburys and Tesco, or Dr. Smart's and Sister Bright's private hospitals - but as points of entry to the social or health or other services. It follows that if they are to respond to this trust they must know their place in the wider field, know what others have to offer, and refer people on if necessary. It implies a professional approach, though the word 'profession' is unfortunately losing some of its status these days.

What applies in the field of personal services also applies at national and less personal levels. If there are organisations which overlap they owe it

to their clients to know and to take account of what
the others are doing: and where there are statutory
services also, the same applies. We shall examine
our sample organisations to see what the situation
is, under these two heads, relations with other
voluntary bodies and relations with statutory
agencies.

RELATIONS WITH OTHER VOLUNTARY BODIES

The professional approach, called for above,
specifies a common base of knowledge, and a common
concern for the client, which should be found
amongst organisations in similar fields. We have
discussed part of the subject of knowledge in
Chapters 3 and 4,in respect of sound information and
expertise, and close understanding of the needs of
the client or consumer. We have seen that in some
organisations there is scope for considerable
improvement in these respects.
        Knowledge must also be of organisations doing
the same work i.e. which are supplementary to one
another; or having different roles, i.e. which
complement one another. It must lead to a concern
to exchange views and experiences where these seem
to lead to different precepts or practices, so that
they can either be resolved or explained without
rancour to those outside. If it appears to the man-
in-the-street that there are several organisations
doing the same work for no good reason, or that
their attitudes or policies conflict, or that they
compete for support with no regard for others in the
field, this can only do harm to the work as a whole,
and indeed to voluntary movements in general.
        One of the requests put to those in the sample
was to name the organisations working in the same or
overlapping fields. As was expected, certain of the
sample named a large number: the Church Army for
example, because the scope of its work is so much
greater than most; and CCE because almost any
benevolent fund is by definition in the same field.
In many cases there were marginal organisations,
whose overlap was slight or of questionable
importance, and we will ignore these. So far as the
others are concerned, overlaps will normally occur
only with part of the activity of an organisation
and only rarely could it be said that the whole of
its work was covered by another body. Even if
several organisations are listed the total amount of
overlap may be quite small. The results are set out
in Appendix G.

Of the 18 organisations in our sample:

2	mentioned	1	organisation(s)	overlapping
3	"	2	"	"
7	"	3	"	"
2	"	4	"	"
4	"	6	"	"

The median number of organisations overlapping is 3.
The sample organisations were then asked whether there were any areas of conflict with other bodies. The answer was 'yes' only in five cases: in all of them there was a difference of view on a matter of policy, recent examples being:

1. Between BDA and the National Deaf Children's Society on educational methods.
2. Between CHAR and the Salvation Army over the future of large hostels.
3. Between CA and CHAR on the same issue.
4. Between NAWCH and the Patients Association over attitudes to hospitalisation.
5. Between NGEC and the National Gypsy Council over 'designation' of gypsy sites; and the Advisory Council for the Education of Romanies and other Travellers (ACERT) on educational policy for gypsies.

All these were significant differences of opinion, genuinely held, and it would perhaps be surprising if such differences did not exist where organisations are deeply involved in their fields of work. The important thing is that dialogue should take place so that issues can be resolved in the course of time rather than lead to entrenched hostility. In only two cases did I feel that the latter was possible.
There were also differences due to competition, in three cases over applications or appeals for funds, and in one case because it was felt that a fellow organisation was trying to 'hog the field' of a certain kind of provision, when a sharing would have been helpful. Competition for funds was felt to be inevitable at times, but there were clear feelings too that it should be minimised by consultation and it was interesting later to be told by the DHSS that the larger organisations coming there for funds 'seem to sort things out' beforehand so as to avoid competition. Competition between organisations wanting to provide the same service may however point to a deeper antagonism.

Members of the sample were also asked whether they had experienced criticism from the public of the fact that there were, or appeared to be, several organisations in the same field. There was very little positive response to this, and where there was it was accompanied by a vigorous assertion that such criticism was not justified, either because there were significant differences of role for the several bodies concerned (asserted by BDA and FEGH) or because uniformity was not a virtue (NGEC).

What then were the ways in which liaison was achieved, if at all, by the organisations in the sample, with those in the same or overlapping fields? The first point to make is that, with possibly one exception, it is not done by cross-representation on committees. Even if that were regarded as a satisfactory method, which it probably would not be, it happened only rarely and then mostly because a person had been individually elected or recruited by more than one body. Nor is it achieved by some action taken by the National Council for Voluntary Organisations, whose role in co-ordination used to be emphasised in days gone by, though less so now. Only JGAD and NAWCH mentioned that they had representatives on specialist groups convened by NCVO, and only NAWCH did so as an indication of how liaison was achieved.

Only three of the sample categorically stated that no liaison was achieved with others in the field. The first was FEGH, which had 'no time' for it, and is not even in membership of the intermediary body for the elderly, Age Concern England: though committee members interviewed stressed the willingness of FEGH to be co-operative if approached by other organisations. Then there was MHA, which said that there was 'no need' for such liaison, for which claim the case seems strong in that the likelihood of any significant overlap with its work seems very small indeed: it was not however a member of the National Federation of Housing Associations, from which intermediary it would have seemed likely at least to get some benefit. Finally, there was HCT, and this was more surprising in that it would seem likely that common cause could often have been made with benefit on some issues with the National Federation of Housing Associations on the one hand, or Shelter on the other. It can safely be assumed that they read one anothers' journals but is that enough?

Of the remaining fifteen, RADAR is an intermediary body, in business to provide liaison, and will be discussed as such later; and nine claimed that liaison was achieved mainly in informal ways. They were:

CHSA   Agreement not to make research grants for heart research because other bodies do so.

CA   Co-operates on particular projects e.g. with the Salvation Army on 'Out in the cold' campaign. Staff attend meetings at least one a year of 15 organisations in contiguous fields of work.

CCE   Co-operate in case work with other casework agencies.

FNF

JGAD

MHCAA

NGEC   Though informal liaison was said to be achieved with the Romany Guild and the Association of Gypsy Organisations, there was no liaison at all with the National Gypsy Council.

SHA   Specially close liaison at officer and committee member level with National Association for the Care and Resettlement of Offenders (NACRO).

WEA

It is interesting that three of these were members of intermediary bodies covering their own fields but did not regard this as worthy of special mention in the context of 'liaison':   they were:

JGAD   which is affiliated to RADAR.

MHCAA   which is affiliated to National Council of Voluntary Child Care Organisations (NCVCCO).

SHA   which is affiliated to National Federation of Housing Associations.

On the other hand, another of the sample, Sh. H. & A. spoke very positively about their liaison with others being fully and satisfactorily achieved by membership of the NCVCCO.

There remain four others to be mentioned. One is NAWCH, which is the one possible exception to the claim that liaison is not achieved by cross-representation on committees. Its Director was on the Executive Committee of the National Children's Bureau (NCB); another member of NAWCH was on the Voluntary Organisations Liaison Council for Under-

Fives (VOLCUF); and NAWCH is a member of the NCVO
Health and Handicapped Group. Between them
these memberships may provide some of what is
required, though they do not for example, cover the
activities of the Patients Association with which,
as we have seen earlier, NAWCH was in disagreement
over attitudes to hospitalisation. Strange as it
may seem, there is no intermediary body concerned
with the National Health Service as a whole to which
bodies like NAWCH could affiliate for mutual
knowledge and benefit.

The other three are organisations whose liaison
with others in their fields is more formalised;
they are BDA, CHAR and RBLHA. Taking these in
reverse order, RBLHA is a member not only of NFHA
but also of the '5,000 group', of housing
associations which have 5,000 or more units of
accommodation; this is really an informal extension
of the intermediary body's liaison role. CHAR,
though itself in some ways an intermediary body, is
a member of the Joint Charities Group on
Homelessness, which has fifteen organisations in it,
but it seems that the group's effectiveness may have
declined as it grew and is now regarded as of less
value in liaison than informal contact. BDA is a
member of the 'panel of four' organisations for the
deaf. This is an interesting group in that it was
brought together by Sir Keith Joseph when he was
Secretary of State for Social Services. It meets
the Minister once every nine months and members also
meet at other times. This seems to have been a case
where there was no intermediary body which the DHSS
could meet, so some coming together was called for;
neither BDA nor the other three major organisations
for the deaf had joined RADAR.

The general impression that one is left with on
the matter of liaison with others is that, with the
odd exception such as FEGH and MHA, there is a
reasonably extensive knowledge of what others in the
field are doing. Largely this is achieved
informally, though more formal organisations whether
full-blooded specialist intermediary bodies such as
RADAR, NCVCCO, ACE or NFHA, or others such as the
'panel of four', have a part to play; real liaison
however is a matter involving more intimacy and
detail than can be achieved by the inevitably
occasional meetings that intermediary bodies call.

Affiliation

It is appropriate here to refer to a request put to

all our sample asking for a list of bodies to which the organisation was affiliated. The intention was to discuss what were the wider fields in which each of them played some part, and in particular what intermediary bodies there were in these fields. The former aim was successful, but the lists obtained clearly comprised a number of bodies which were not in the Wolfenden sense intermediary i.e. bringing all or most of the organisations together in a federal way. Appendix H details the lists obtained, which are summarised quantitatively in Table 5.1.

Table 5.1: Number of bodies to which organisations are affiliated

No. of affiliations	No. of organisations
None	5
One	6
Two	2
Three	–
Four	2
Five	–
Six	1
Seven and over	2

There were eight organisations affiliated to NCVO. These apart, the interest of the lists is in those which had none or one affiliation and, at the other end of the scale, those which had a considerable number. Thus, of the former, we find:

BDA   no affiliation except NCVO.

CHSA   no affiliation, perhaps indicating that there is no intermediary body in health education or medical research in its particular field.

CCE   not officially affiliated to, but 'close relationship' with, Age Concern England.

FNF   affiliated only to Family Forum.

FEGH   no affiliation: as we have seen, it has not sought any liaison with others.

HCT   no affiliation except NCVO, perhaps because there is no intermediary body in housing, but also because it is a membership, if not an intermediary, body itself.

MHA   no affiliation, again an organisation not seeking liaison.

NGEC   no affiliation, perhaps because there is no intermediary body for gypsy organisations.

RADAR   no affiliation but NCVO, but itself an
intermediary body by any definition.
RBLHA   affiliated only to the National Federation
of Housing Associations.
Sh.H&A   affiliated only to National Council of
Voluntary Child Care Organisations.
WEA   affiliated to NCVO and National Institute of
Adult Eduction.

All these organisations apparently saw little
reason to affiliate to bodies other than those very
closely covering their field of work. Three at the
other end of the scale seemed to use affiliation not
only for liaison and joint action but also for
widening the scope of their interest. How else can
one explain the seven affiliations of CHAR, itself
an intermediary body anyway; the eleven affiliations
of NAWCH; or the six of SHA? Some of the bodies
concerned are intermediary, such as MIND or NACRO;
some are on a par with HCT i.e. study and membership
bodies, such as the National Children's Bureau; but
others seem to be neither, such as the National
Cyrenians or Fair Play for Children.

Nevertheless this examination of liaison and
affiliation points to an astonishing number of
intermediary bodies, witnessing to the wide
diversity of activity undertaken by voluntary
organisations. Though these can only be a part of
the spectrum, seen as they are through the eyes of a
sample of national organisations, we would expect to
net a substantial proportion of the total if our
initial sample was truly representative, but what
the proportion is we have no means of knowing. Nor
have we any indication of the functions and standing
of some of them. Six were not listed either in the
NCVO Directory of Voluntary Organisations nor in the
London telephone directory: it seems that these may
be small essentially back-up organisations, known to
those that affiliate to them, but not courting a
public image. Some, such as the Maternity Alliance,
may be solely campaign organisations.

The list of 'intermediary' bodies thrown up by
our sample was as follows:

Family Forum
National Council of Voluntary Organisations   (NCVO)
National Association for the Care and
Resettlement of Offenders   (NACRO)
National Association for Mental Health   (MIND)
Campaign for the Single Homeless   (CHAR)
Council of Voluntary Welfare Work (Forces)   (CWW)

Royal Association for Disability and
Rehabilitation   (RADAR)
Holiday Care Association
National Council of Voluntary Child Care
Organisations   (NCVCCO)
British Association of Adoption and
Fostering Agencies
Voluntary Organisations Liaison Council
for Under Fives   (VOLCUF)
Play in Hospital Liaison Committee
National Council of Women   (NCW)
Standing Conference of Women's Organisations
Maternity Alliance
Independent Council for the Mentally
Handicapped
National Federation of Housing Associations   (NFHA)
National Association of Voluntary Hostels   (NAVH)
National Institute of Adult Education   (NIAE)

One of the intermediary bodies referred to in
interviews with our sample organisations, NCVCCO,
was so well commended, for one reason or another, by
at least three of them, that it seemed worthwhile to
find out a little more about it, and to compare it
with other intermediary organisations in our
sample.

Intermediary Bodies

The Wolfenden Committee, the chief protagonist
of intermediary bodies, indeed the inventor of the
description, listed the main functions of local
intermediary bodies as:

a)   Development - reviewing existing provision,
     identifying current needs and initiating action
     to meet them, seeing where duplication exists
     and trying to achieve a better match between
     needs and resources
b)   Services to other organisations
c)   Liaison - defined as the exchange of
     information and opinion between organisations
d)   Representation - articulating views, protecting
     interests, pressing for changes through
     negotiations, and publicity, on behalf of the
     organisations represented
e)   Direct services to individuals.

The committee added that the list is not in order of
priority, nor is it suggested that all such bodies
carry out all of them.(2) Later it stated that most

of the activities of independent <u>national</u> intermediary bodies fall into the same classification of
functions.(3)

The question how wide 'a field' is may be like
the proverbial 'How long is a piece of string?' The
need for liaison, as we have seen, grows when only
two or three bodies are operating in the same field,
and this may be met by the simplest of informal
groupings, but there comes a time or a range of
activity when the number of organisations is such
that a more formal association is inevitable if the
same objects are to be achieved. In our sample CHAR
is an intermediary body in that it has 150 member
organisations in the campaign for the single
homeless; and RADAR is intermediary for 400
organisations concerned with disability. The body
to which several of our sample are affiliated,
NCVCCO, has 45 member organisations in child care.

There is no doubt that NCVCCO was most
appreciated for the advice and information it was
able to give the smaller organisations; and for
representing them in relations with government. It
is interesting that NCVCCO has advice and
information functions though, unlike CHAR and RADAR,
it undertakes no systematic accumulation of
information. It depends entirely on the CEO's
personal knowledge and wisdom, which in turn must
depend on his extensive contacts with his own member
organisations and with government.

Contacts with his own members are indeed close.
NCVCCO has a Council with representatives from
member organisations as follows:

Staff employed	Representation
1,000 or more	4
500 or more	2
under 500	1

It meets at least twice a year. It has a General
Purposes Committee on which the 'big four' - large
national societies having extensive regional and/or
local constituencies - have permanent places, all
occupied by CEOs and therefore people of great
professional knowledge and experience. When it
prepares its views, for example for DHSS, first
thoughts are put by its CEO to all members and
possibly to regional groups of members; this is
followed by another short paper for discussion by
the General Purposes Committee, and then a draft
statement is circulated again to all members for

further comment. Only then is the final draft
prepared. Comments on green papers and other
consultative documents are frequent, as is the case
in CHAR and RADAR.

Relationships with government and Parliament
are also close. NCVCCO has an observer from DHSS
Social Work Service on its General Purposes
Committee, whose attendance is unfailing, and RADAR
has several observers though CHAR has none. The CEO
has easy and frequent access at professional, policy
and political levels to DHSS, and at times (mostly
via interdepartmental machinery) to other government
departments: CHAR and RADAR would claim the same.
NCVCCO is represented on an all-party parliamentary
group, as are both the other organisations. At
local government level, NCVCCO has regular meetings
with the Association of Directors of Social Services
(ADSS); CHAR has 'relaxed' relationships with LBA
and GLC, but unfortunately a less warm relationship
with AMA; and RADAR has an ADSS observer on its
committee, as well as having many local authorities
in membership.

All three organisations get grants from central
government. In the case of NCVCCO the grant pays
the salary of the CEO, and as the staff consists
only of himself and a part-time secretary the grant
is very significant, 56% of income. For CHAR, as we
have seen in Chapter 3, it is 70% and for RADAR 41%.
That having been said, however, a word of wonder is
appropriate for NCVCCO, a) because the organisation
is (with apologies to the secretary) of the nature
of one man and his dog, and b) because member
organisations are prepared to pay substantial
subscriptions to it. ('Category A' subscriptions -
large national societies - are £1,260 p.a.).

NCVCCO does not concern itself greatly with the
politics of child care, explaining this partly with
the phrase that it 'doesn't bite the hand that
feeds it'. This is not wholly convincing, for both
CHAR and RADAR apparently feel free to do so.
Indeed CHAR's raison d'etre is to concern itself
with policy and political matters. It is accepted
in NCVCCO that member organisations, notably 'the
big four', may make their own representations to
government, which may not accord with the NCVCCO
corporate line, and political and wider social
policy matters may be channelled to government in
that way. This may at times apply also to members
of CHAR and RADAR.

A field of activity of an intermediary body,
wider though it is by definition than that of many

other organisations, may still not be wide enough
for all purposes. Thus NCVCCO is itself a member of
the National Children's Bureau; CHAR is affiliated
to, or has reciprocal membership arrangements with,
the National Association for the Care and
Resettlement of Offenders (NACRO) and with Shelter;
and even RADAR, broad though its base is, was seeing
a need for an even broader affiliation in the
Snowdon Council for Disabled People, arising out of
the International Year of Disabled People 1981.

The position of NCVO, seen through the eyes of
our sample, is ambiguous. As we have seen, NAWCH
quoted the NCVO Health and Handicapped Group as
a means of keeping in touch with other bodies in
that field: on the other hand NCVCCO resented the
tactlessness of NCVO in forming a child care group
without consulting it (NCVCCO) and did not think
such a group was needed. The majority opinion in
the sample certainly was that the proper role, and
the strength, of NCVO is dealing with issues common
to all voluntary organisations regardless of field
of activity, issues such as VAT and charity law to
take two topical examples.

From our brief look at NCVCCO it seems that
perhaps the paramount value of the intermediary body
is that it helps those affiliated to it to build up
a united front on issues important to them, and acts
as a channel to and from statutory agencies, which
are represented by observers on their committees,
and with which close contact is always established.
This is much appreciated by many of the constituent
bodies, particularly the smaller ones; but we have
also seen that not all organisations are able to
maintain liaison with statutory activity in this
way.

We have examined how far they are in touch with
their voluntary colleagues. We must now examine
their relationships with statutory agencies in more
detail.

RELATIONSHIP WITH STATUTORY AGENCIES

In this section of the chapter we are able to draw
not only on what we learnt from the sample
organisations but also from interviews with staff of
the government departments relating to those
organisations' work. Interviews in the main were
not about specific organisations, but about general
attitudes and policies towards voluntary bodies.

Where provision of services is concerned, first
there is the fact that voluntary and statutory

agencies are involved in a considerable number of similar activities: and second, that certain activities of voluntary organisations are regarded as particularly valuable by statutory agencies, though the latter do not for one reason or another undertake them themselves.

Common activities have been illustrated already in Table 3.1. Residential homes and hostels, social work, youth centres, health education, housing, holidays, adoption, intermediate treatment and adult education, are all within the programmes of both voluntary and statutory. The Barclay report saw unmet possibilities in this:

> The voluntary sector is potentially an equal partner with the statutory in the planning and provision of services, but, in our view, the relationship to date between the two sectors could seldom be described as a genuine partnership. It sometimes resembles that between statutory master and voluntary servant.(4)

This comment appears to have particular validity perhaps in the context of governmment funding of voluntary organisations, for even the most independent-minded seeker of funds is bound to feel a modicum of servility, if only for short periods, when negotiations are going on. The NCVO reports that the Conservative government of 1979-83 increased programme financing for voluntary organi- sations very considerably, that assistance from the DHSS towards the central costs has also expanded, but that 'as voluntary organisations increased their dependence on government money, so government began to take a closer look at what it was paying for'.(5) One third of our sample received government funds for general purposes, and in four cases the grants comprised more than 50% of the organisation's total income.

It is clear from interviews with government departments that for some the major reason for any contact with voluntary organisations is the fact that grants are made to them. Especially was this so for DES and the Home Office. The DES said that they had no real contact with organisations that do not receive grant aid, (HMI contacts with educat- ional institutions presumably excepted), and the Home Office almost repeated this, though adding that they do have 'a dialogue' with certain others. The DoE and the DHSS liked to have other contacts, 'to

keep our ear to the ground', but kept particularly
close where grants were made. The responses from
the sample organisations bear out what the departments said, for it was only those that get grants
for general purposes that spoke of a close relationship with government administrators. NAWCH, RADAR
and SHA have observers on their committees (from
five departments in the case of RADAR); though CHAR
and WEA do not.

In all cases there is apparently a flow of
information, at least every other week, between
these organisations and departments, more from
former to latter than the other way if we are to
believe the replies received from the sample.
Mostly the exchange is by telephone. Information
exchange also takes place with HCT, though this is
one of our sample that does not get a grant. At
times a department that is undertaking a piece of
research in a particular field, or is preparing, for
example, a code of guidance, will work the voluntary
organisation quite hard for a short time. In this
case the information received is no doubt carefully
digested, though departments were a little cautious
in the replies to the general question as to whether
information received was fed back into their own
intelligence systems: the answer was in effect
'yes, but perhaps not as systematically as it might
be'.

There were fairly close contacts at professional as opposed to administrative level in three or
four other cases, e.g. with HMIs at the DES, (NGEC
had an HMI observer on its committee), technical
advisers at the DoE, or the Social Work Service at
DHSS. The DES itself made a point of the value of
having the HMI around as 'mediator' or 'honest
broker' between organisations and the department's
administrators: and the Home Office less strongly
ascribed a similar role to the Probation Service or
Inspectorate.

The reasons why departments were pleased to
have observers on the committees of certain
voluntary organisations, were to see how thinking is
developing and pick up ideas and problems at an
early stage, though one department said there were
only two organisations in its field where it was
really worthwhile. Other departments made it clear
that in practice they could not send observers to as
many committees as they would like, Three out of
the four main departments were against allowing
staff to serve on voluntary committees when invited
in a personal capacity: exceptions were

occasionally made but 'clearance' by the department was a 'delicate decision' and would only be given if there was no financial involvement of the department in the organisation's work.

Departments made a point of meeting organisations to which they make grants about once a year, to look at reports and accounts and discuss the work. Government auditors may go in if the department considers it necessary. CHAR regarded its written reports to departments as opportunities to inform them of developments as much as to account for use of money. DES, whose grants range from quite small (£15,000 p.a.) to quite large (£1 million p.a.), referred to their close interest in how the money is spent, but their anxiety about organisations which depend on grants for more than half their income.

Involvement of voluntary organisations with government policy concerns the pressure groups mostly, and the methods of 'social advocacy' they use have been listed in Chapter 3. One of these is submissions to committees of enquiry of all sorts, and in some cases organisations, or individuals associated with them, are invited by departments to serve on such committees. Four of our sample had been involved in this way, and all of the government departments seen favoured this process, though adding that committees were not set up so frequently under the present government, and that invitations inevitably had to be very selective. One former senior civil servant told the author that representation is invited 'for tactical reasons in that there are distinguished figures and important experience in the voluntary field to offset the statutory interests, and the voluntary organisations cannot be ignored as they help the economy and have influence in Parliament'. The Home Office particularly favoured what it described as 'working groups', serviced by the department, often chaired by an officer of the Probation Service, though these would be more concerned with technical matters than with policy.

Views of organisations were sought on Green Papers, consultative documents, draft Bills and circulars etc. - half of our sample responded on these matters occasionally, some quite often - but it was pointed out both by departments and by organisations that 'Ministers' (is it really them?) often want replies more quickly than the procedures of voluntary organisations allow. Getting the 'overall' views of the voluntary organisations in

one particular field was 'difficult at times', said
one department, and so views received were often not
comprehensive or constructive.

It is interesting to read what others have said
about the influence of voluntary bodies on
departmental policies: Ian Bradley found that 'It
is almost impossible to obtain a Civil Service view
of the power and effectiveness of pressure groups',
but he went on:

> A former Home Office official says that he
> would rate the most important influences on
> policy as first, professional associations;
> second, pressure groups; third, academics; and
> fourth, MPs. (6)

Other writers differ on how far government
takes account of outside groups: Walkland belittles
the influences of 'attitude' or promotional groups,
whilst admitting that there is 'a general consensus
on the legitimacy of organised interests having a
voice in public policy', (7) whereas Wootton bemoans
that 'Almost like Gulliver in the toils of the
Lilliputians, Leviathan may be seriously hampered by
the many groups clustered around it'.(8) Between
these two assessments comes the calmer judgment of
Windlesham - 'Often the government has to rely upon
the voluntary organisations to provide the
specialist knowledge which alone can make new
legislation relevant or effective' (9) - and this
was also the conclusion of Hall et al. (10) We need
to remember too that as many as three out of our six
organisations getting government grants were formed
with governmental encouragement - CHAR, SHA, and
RADAR at whose birth, the DHSS explained, the
Department was 'midwife'. There must be some family
feeling somewhere.

So far we have referred only to the
administrators in government departments, but,
particularly so far as pressure groups are
concerned, voluntary bodies look also to the
political heads of departments and to members of
parliament for support and consultation, and it
seems that they in turn may need what these bodies
can give them. According to Moodie and Studdert-
Kennedy:

> The normal condition of the politician is one
> of uncertainty about the nature and strength of
> the claims on his representation role, about
> the impact of his own and his colleagues'

> behaviour on different publics. But whatever
> his ideological or partisan confidence, he is
> in constant need of digestible information, in
> the first instance to increase his control over
> his own options and prospective survival and
> success, and in the second to perform his role
> as a representative, exercising his better
> judgment on behalf of others.(11)

Barker and Rush tell us that 'there is clearly a
need felt by Members for some of the material sent
them by organised interest groups', (12) and
Englefield that in the House of Commons Library
sources of Reference Sheets and Background Papers
prepared by library staff for MPs 'are mostly a wide
range of official papers, including statistics,
authoritative political publications, journal
articles and press comment, <u>pressure group</u>
<u>literature</u>, etc.'(13) (My underlining.)

Government departments all emphasised that the
influence which a voluntary organisation has depends
in a major way on how well its case is presented.
Factually accurate material - 'not half-baked' as
one department candidly put it - from an organisation with a reputation for being reliable, and with
an application that can immediately be seen to be
relevant, will have most effect. It also helps if
the organisation has the support of Ministers and
MPs and also of people professional to the field
concerned. 'How loud they shout' is not an insigni-
ficant factor, but they must also know when to <u>stop</u>
pressing the case. In our sample, six organis<u>ations</u>
met Ministers from time to time, formally or informally, four of them once a year or more frequently.
A few, as Chapter 3 has indicated, also have regular
contacts with individual MPs or with All-Party
Parliamentary Committees.

The impressions given from all sides are
consistently of a fairly ready exchange of
information and views between organisations
receiving grant aid and the departments providing
it, and of some influence being exerted on policy by
these and by a few others. There are the inevitable
complaints that the people who maintain the contact
for government departments are moved on to other
work irritatingly soon after stable relationships
have been established, and the answer comes back
that organisations should not place so much emphasis
on <u>people</u>, and look more to <u>roles</u>. This is to
ignore the fact, that cannot be avoided, that
personalities do matter: where it could be said of

one Assistant Secretary that 'She always made you feel you'd said too much, even if it was only "Good morning"', relationships could not have been as good as they would have been had the person concerned been of warmer disposition. Nevertheless, for perhaps two-thirds of our sample, a positive relationship existed. It is for the other third for which there was no such relationship that questions must be raised. Do they go their way without taking any account of one another, the voluntary and the statutory, and if so does this matter?

A closer look at the organisations concerned leads to different answers in different cases. There are three categories, which may be illustrated by two of our sample in each case. First, there are those who seem to relate to government, very adequately for their size, through intermediary bodies. These are illustrated by MHCAA, affiliated as we have seen to the British Association of Adoption and Fostering Agencies and the National Council of Voluntary Child Care Organisations, and also, incidentally, as most of its child care work is in the London area, to local intermediary bodies; and Sh. H & A., also affiliated to NCVCCO in a very positive way.

Second, there are those which go their own way largely because that way is rather singular, illustrated by FNF and MHA. In fact FNF is affiliated to Family Forum, and does have quite helpful contacts with the Law Commission and the High Court of Justice, which may set its campaign well into context, though I could not judge this. MHA is doing work hardly any other body is doing, and has in any case been solely a management organisation for many years now. There is probably little to question in either of these cases.

The third group is rather different, illustrated by CHSA and FEGH. Neither has any affiliation or any evident relationship with government (though CHSA did refer to a 'special understanding' with the Health Education Council) yet both are working in fields where there is much voluntary and statutory activity. There is no doubt in my mind that for them to take so little account of what others are doing, and vice versa, can only be a loss all round.

We have been discussing contacts between national organisations and central government. A mention should also be made of contacts with 'local government' in the broadest sense, which would be effected largely through the local government associations, Association of County Councils (ACC), Association of Metropolitan Authorities (AMA), and Association of District Councils (ADC).

These associations nominate members to a number of national voluntary organisations operating in fields in which the authorities have some responsibility e.g. in education or child care for the counties; in housing or access for the disabled for districts. Such representation is however very patchy and, perhaps inevitably, far from comprehensive: as is the reporting back of the local authority representatives to those who nominate them. Otherwise there are informal meetings from time to time on particular areas of concern, largely between officers, and occasionally these lead to joint action. All in all, however, the contacts at this level cannot be said to be great.

PARTNERS OR RIVALS?

The provisional conclusions of the various parts of this chapter so far have been:

a) that voluntary organisations in the same or overlapping fields have in the main a reasonably full knowledge of what others are doing and that this is mostly achieved informally

b) that there is some competition for funds and occasional clashes of policy, but that intense rivalries which could jeopardise their work are rare

c) that for a few there is quite extensive affiliation to other organisations to widen the context of their work

d) that intermediary bodies are of value particularly in providing information and a dialogue with statutory authorities for their member organisations

e) that for about three-quarters of our sample a positive relationship existed between voluntary organisations and relevant central government agencies. We noted, too, in Chapter 1, that central government departments find some voluntary organisations of real value in the provision of service, information or agitation which they would not or could not undertake themselves, though they do not, and/or would not wish to, have close contacts with others

f) that there is co-operation with local authority associations in some fields but that this is far from comprehensive.

The reader may conclude from this that the answer to the question at the head of this section is that partnership predominates over rivalry. This would be correct but does beg the question of what partnership is. Is it enough for voluntary organisations to know what others are doing, and to take avoiding action if conflict appears imminent? Is there a real understanding on the part of voluntary and statutory of how the other functions and what it can or cannot reasonably be expected to do? Is there agreement between those providing services on the roles of each in a specified programme, whether the one supplements the other or makes a different but complementary provision? Is there meaningful discussion of social policy between service and pressure groups and politicians or Whitehall policy-makers?
    If partnership is couched in these terms the conclusions are distinctly less optimistic. Fortnightly talks on the telephone may help to resolve particular problems for services in the field, and might possibly bring to light some of the major policy issues lying behind the work, but cannot possibly go further. 'Views' sought by government departments were on drafts of documents already prepared and were wanted often at too short notice. Working parties referred to were on practical issues, and committees of enquiry are rare and exclusive. Once yearly meetings to consider the government grant could do little more than just that. Nowhere was there any indication of a longer-term meeting of minds, and further consideration must be given to this in our final chapter. First however we must look at another aspect of government grant, the requirements of 'accountability', and also go on to a more comprehensive view of what that word means.

REFERENCES

1. Bottome, Phyllis. London Pride. Faber and
        Faber, London, 1941.
2. The future of voluntary organisations, (p.110).
        Croom Helm, London, 1978.
3. Op cit. (p.129).

4. Social Workers: their role and tasks. Report
     of the Barclay Committee, (p.85). Bedford
     Square Press, London, 1982.
5. Editorial in Voluntary Action, Summer 1983.
6. Bradley, Ian. In The Times, April 9, 1980.
7. Walkland, S. A. The Legislative Process in
     Great Britain, (Chapter III). George
     Allen and Unwin, London, 1968.
8. Wootton, Graham. Pressure Politics in Contemp-
     orary Britain. Lexington Books, D.C.
     Heath and Co., Lexington, Massachusetts,
     1978.
9. Windlesham, Lord. Politics in Practice,
     (p.76). Jonathan Cape, London, 1975.
10. Hall, Land, Parker and Webb. Change, Choice
     and Conflict in Social Policy, (Ch.6).
     Heinemann Educational Books, London, 1975.
11. Moodie G. C. and Studdert-Kennedy, G. Opinions,
     Publics and Pressure Groups, (p.97).
     George Allen and Unwin, London, 1970.
12. Barker, A. and Rush, M. The Member of
     Parliament and his Information, (p.67).
     George Allen and Unwin, London, 1970.
13. Englefield, Dermot. Parliament and Informa-
     tion, (p.44). Library Association
     Publishing, London, 1981.

Chapter 6

ACCOUNTABILITY

> It is even harder to grapple with the concept
> of accountability. Its popularity in the human
> services is exceeded only by the lack of agree-
> ment about its meaning. It has been viewed as
> both an end and a means; it has been defined in
> terms of procedures, results, disclosure
> of information, recourse, and compliance with
> regulations; and it is often indistinguishable
> from such concepts as evaluation, efficiency,
> effectiveness, control and responsibility.
>
> - Voluntary Agencies in the Welfare State
>   (Ralph M. Kramer)

That there is lack of agreement about the meaning of
the word 'accountability' was evident from the
responses made by the sample organisations, to the
question about how they were meeting requirements in
this respect. Six of them thought of accountability
to their own membership; five to the government or
local government departments from which they
obtained funds; and another five, to their subscribers and supporters. Only one (MHA) referred to its
'consumers', i.e. those for whom it provided accommodation: and it was noteworthy that only one
organisation referred to the Charity Commission,
though two housing associations (RBLHA and SHA)
mentioned the Housing Corporation in its supervisory
(as opposed to its funding) role.
    The Concise Oxford Dictionary definition of
'accountable' is: 'Bound to give account,
responsible (for things, to persons....)'
Being 'bound' is much narrower than many of the
sample see accountability. It implies legal
obligations. Being 'responsible' however, goes
further. In this chapter we will examine various
headings of accountability, in what the author
regards as an order of priority, and look both at
legal obligations and a wider approach under each
heading. Under some of them there will be subheadings.

1. To meet their responsibilities as corporate
    bodies.

It is hardly necessary to state that such bodies

must conform to the laws of the land, in particular
as employers or landlords. They also have their own
laws written specially for them. They must therefore:

a) Adhere to the terms of trust, memorandum of
   association, or other statement of objects;
b) Comply with the rules, articles or other statements of procedure laid down by law.

From these it follows that they must also:

c) Adopt broad policies in conformity with these
   requirements within which staff employed (if
   any) must work;
d) Satisfy members whoever they are, that these
   things are so.

These are more than legal formalities, in that
many organisations were provided when established
with such broad statements of aims and powers of
action that it would be quite difficult not to
conform, and therefore a contemporary interpretation
of what is required is significant and it is this
that must be communicated for approval to the
membership. Items c) and d) therefore assume a
particular importance.

As has been stated, several of our sample
thought first of their members. We have already
referred in Chapter 3 (page 63) to the 'grass-roots'
influence on policy making noted by some; and in
Chapter 4 to the variations in the meaning of
membership; in the degree of its involvement in the
election of committees, and in the extent to which
policies are submitted to it.

Specifically on accountability, BDA referred to
its Annual Reports (though in fact recent ones were
not available at the time of enquiry) and to a
'lively movement and election procedure': and CHAR
expressed itself as 'excessively pre-occupied' with
membership views and mentioned its three general
meetings each year. RADAR, however saw little
reality in the idea of accountability to members:
though it was confident that 'if anything went badly
wrong someone would pick it up and take action upon
it', beyond that there was 'no practical
accountability'. Once the committee had been
elected, responsibility lay with it and it alone,
seemed to be the burden of RADAR's response.

This may be fair comment where service
organisations are concerned but it is strongly
arguable that accountability to members has special

importance where the organisation seeks to
represent a particular category of people or to
facilitate mutual aid. Mutual aid organisations as
such have been excluded from our field of study, but
in our sample there are five at least which could be
said to make claims to representing a particular
category. They are BDA, CHAR, FNF, NAWCH and NGEC,
and in Chapter 4 (p.86) we concluded that all these
were notably democratic in their election
procedures, i.e. notably responsive to members in
this way at least.
    The responsibility to satisfy members is dealt
with further in 2b) below. In general, however, it
may be concluded that those in our sample were
meeting their responsibilities under this heading of
accountability.

2.   To use funds available in accordance with
      purposes for which they were provided.

There are numerous subheadings according to the
funds concerned.

a)   Legacies and endowments. In these cases the
attachment of funds may be, perhaps normally is, to
the organisation as a whole, in which case the
responsibility is covered by what has been said in
1. above. It may however be to a specific purpose
or function of the organisation and an account must
be kept separate so that funds and their use are
suitably related: the preparation of accounts has
been discussed in Chapter 3.

b)   Subscriptions and donations. Where the term
'subscription' is used to describe a set amount
contributed by a 'member' of the organisation, the
responsibility to subscribers and members is one and
the same. Most organisations also have donations,
by which is meant sums contributed without formality
or corresponding rights, to vote, attend meetings,
receive reports etc. Here we are talking more of
responsibilities than of legal obligations. Whether
we are referring to members or donors the ways of
meeting a responsibility towards them are much the
same. They include Annual Reports, which should be
automatically provided or readily available shortly
after the year in question has ended; and statements
of accounts, clearly set out, and properly audited,
also readily available; occasionally there may be
other ways by which subscribers and donors may be
informed of what is being done, for example by

special meetings arranged for them or to which they
may be invited.

Two organisations made considerable efforts to
keep in touch with their supporters and
subscribers. Perhaps the most active in this
respect was CA, which produced a little journal
called 'Review' as well as its Annual Report, and
which had Officers regularly 'preaching' about the
work of CA; FEGH in a different way made successful
contact with subscribers, inviting them annually to
a social event and getting an attendance of 2 - 300.
One organisation, Sh. H & A, had gone the extra mile
with their subscribers, and consulted them when
changes were being made to the Memorandum and
Articles: and SHA, not only with subscribers but
also with members of local management committees to
consider, 2,000 in all, had 'started a dialogue',
in which a newsletter played a significant part.
They did however add the cautionary comment that
'you can get too democratic and fall into a hole'.

In general it seemed that formal Annual General
Meetings were reasonably well attended (i.e. 50%
membership or more) in one-third of cases; attended
only by a few, mainly committee members, in another
third; and made into wider events and thus
apparently 'well-attended' in the remainder, though
not necessarily by those with a right to vote.

All the sample organisations in our study were
asked as a matter of routine to provide the author
with copies of their most recent Annual Reports and
Accounts. The requests were made at the end of 1981
or the early part of 1982. All but two provided a
report of some sort for a year which ended not more
than one year previous to the request. The two
which could not were BDA, for which the latest
report available was for 1977; and FNF which had
nothing available. WEA's report is biennial, and
two organisations (NGEC and Sh. H & A) did not
produce an Annual Report as such, but incorporated
information in an annual magazine. Most reports
were of booklet size, though the latest NAWCH report
and accounts was only a leaflet.

Accounts were less readily available. Nine
organisations included them with the Annual Report,
but for one of these the accounts were for an
earlier period than the report. Eight of the sample
produced separate Accounts, but for three of these
Accounts were available only for the year previous
to the Report. Reasons were sometimes forthcoming,
but not always convincing. We have already
concluded (Chapter 3) that Accounts could often be

improved in the way they are designed, and it seems
that the speed with which they are produced also
needs attention, so that this particular responsibility may be adequately discharged.

One of our sample had recently suffered a
substantial misappropriation of funds, which had
been the subject of investigation by the Director of
Public Prosecutions. He had, after consideration of
all aspects, decided that no useful purpose would be
served by prosecution, so that the details of how
the defalcation was discovered are not publicly
available. It would be comforting to think that the
appointment of a reputable firm of auditors took
care of the matter, but I doubt whether anyone who
has experienced the 'spot-check' methods perhaps
inevitably used in normal audits would be sure of
this. On the other hand it must in the longer run
make it more likely that fraud will be checked.
Looking slightly outside our field, a report was
prepared by two Inspectors appointed by the Chief
Registrar of Friendly Societies in 1979, on the
affairs of the Grays Building Society: it found
that the secretary/chairman of the Society had
carried out extensive frauds over a long period of
years and referred to 'a consistent failure of
auditors to discharge their professional duties
properly'.

The obverse of this is surely that consistent
attention to auditing duties must be a valuable
safeguard. Our study had no way of identifying how
far this was being attended to, but since it was
undertaken the NCVO has published a consultation
document which states:

> In our view, the current system of accounta-
> bility leaves much to be desired. We agree
> with the view expressed by the Charity Commis-
> sioners that the routine collection and exami-
> nation of annual accounts does not achieve a
> great deal; we believe that the statutory
> requirements to submit accounts should be
> repealed and replaced by (1) a statutory
> requirement on all charities to make accounts
> available to any member of the public on
> request; and (ii) the establishment of a small
> audit team within the Commission which would
> conduct spot checks on randomly selected
> charities (a procedure used with considerable
> success by the Inland Revenue) as well as
> following up complaints etc.(2)

137

c) <u>Grants</u>. Here the initiative inevitably comes
from the organisation making the grant. It has the
right to make whatever conditions it likes on making
the offer, and the body at the receiving end must in
due course take it or leave it on those terms. If
it takes the money, it must conform to the conditions laid down. That could be said to sum up the
issue of accountability in this respect, but this
would be a gross oversimplification.

We have already, in Chapter 5, referred to the
relationships between voluntary organisations and
government agencies from which grants are received.
Accountability there seems to consist of an annual
appointment to discuss a report on the work done
during the past year, and the needs of the following
year; and sometimes an observer from the department
has a place on the organisation's committee. Here
accountability becomes a much more precise concept,
for even though the grant may be for general work
the nature and extent of that work comes under
scrutiny by the department: and where grant aid is
for a particular piece of work the nature of
accountability is even more precise.

Grants may be available from charitable
foundations, or from local or central government.
The crucial issue arises largely where statutory
funds are concerned, and it is how to strike a
balance between the need for accountability and
the need to respect the role of the voluntary
organisation that is accountable. What that role is
must first be agreed, and it could range from total
freedom to do what it likes, to total serfdom to the
statutory agency. Though some such funding agencies
may at times harbour thoughts of voluntary organisations either providing an obedient extension to the
agencies' work, or being completely taken over, it
has been traditional for the majority of funders to
wish to see voluntary bodies maintaining a significant independence.

If that is the case the grantor will
nevertheless generally wish to be assured, in the
case of a grant to general funds, that the grantee
is maintaining a certain general direction in the
work it is doing; or in the case of a grant for a
particular service, or a piece of research, that
these are being carried out with an assured quality
and momentum.

The grantee on the other hand, whilst being
anxious to provide such assurances, will not wish to
feel that its every move is being monitored, that
its own kinds of initiatives are being sapped, that

its own raison d'etre is being distorted. As a
submission to the government's Voluntary Services
Unit put it in 1979:

> The balance between devolving responsibility to
> an independent organisation and controlling/
> instructing that organisation, is a delicate
> one. If the voluntary body is allowed too much
> flexibility and freedom, it may run into
> difficulties; but if there is too much
> supervision and control, the spirit of
> innovation and enterprise may be stifled. And
> in place of the flexible alternative to state
> provision, there may grow up an equally rigid
> sector firmly under government control, either
> providing little variation from the state
> provision or providing little variation between
> separate organisations. The paymaster, who
> pays the piper calls the tune: but if the
> paymaster insists on precisely how the tune is
> played, by whom where and when, then the piper
> may get fed-up and play no tunes at all. And
> if government insists on the same tune being
> played over and over again, and does not allow
> for the piper to use his own talents of
> composition and improvisation, then there will
> be no variety and diversity. In other words,
> too much supervision and control can destroy
> the value of the exercise and prevent the
> voluntary body achieving the objectives
> government requires from it.(3)

Where the level of grant for general purposes
becomes a high percentage of the organisation's
income there are other dangers, not only because of
the organisation's vulnerability on grant reduction
or withdrawal, which is something it must always
face, but because of potential threats from the
accountability lobbies of left or right of the
political spectrum. Thus, for example, one M.P.
demands 'all bodies which receive fifty percent or
more of their income from public funds, whatever
their relationship to central government, should be
made directly and openly accountable to Parliament.'(4) We have seen in Chapter 3 that two of our
sample could fall into this category, CHAR with 70%
of its income from government grants, and NAWCH with
63%, apart from the two housing associations (RBLHA
and SHA) which need government funds to function at
all.

It is pleasing to be able to state that none of

our sample felt that their independence was improperly jeopardised by having to account in agreed ways for government grants. Unfortunately at the very time of writing, April, 1983, an illustration of the way in which the grant-relationship can be abused was provided by the then Minister for Consumer Affairs, who implied that he might withdraw the government grant to the National Association of Citizen's Advice Bureaux at short notice. Processes of accountability for use of grants may reasonably be required of voluntary organisations, and of course government has a right to expect them to behave in responsible ways, but in return these organisations must be able to trust the departments responsible to maintain the grants for the period agreed, unless very serious breaches of faith have occurred.

d) Rents, fees and charges. At first sight it may seem that these are sources of funds for whose use the only responsibility on the organisation is to provide quid pro quo. There is a little more to it than that. Some of our sample were responsible for providing rented accommodation, and this gives them responsibility to their tenants in ways rather different from the grocer's obligation to the purchaser of a pound of sugar. The Housing Act 1980 introduced a new package of rights for public sector tenants, known as The Tenant's Charter, and housing associations are obliged for example, to publish their tenancy selection and allocation policies, provide certain information to their tenants, and consult tenants when they propose a change in their housing management practice or policy. There are other ways in which a good housing association may 'reach out' to their tenants, such as helping them to form tenants' associations, publishing a newsletter or offering them membership of the Association itself.

Similar opportunities, though no legal obligations, arise where voluntary organisations are providing residential accommodation e.g. in old peoples' homes; or other services, e.g. adoption. Fees are taken for some of these and not for others, but there can be no doubt that the 'clients' in all such cases will often be better served and more satisfied if they are taken into the confidence of the organaisation, and that the latter will gain by feedback from clients into policy making. We have already seen that MHA has an Annual Meeting for its residents; another example is provided by MHCAA,

which does the same for its adoptive parents.
    Where charges for goods are concerned,
the responsibilities are different again, but they
are certainly there. Organisations selling
literature are not providing reading simply to while
away the time: they are providing information and
must get it right. Just as quality of service is
important, so is quality of information: and this
is so not only for service organisations but also,
perhaps more so, for pressure groups. Patrick Seyd
examined the work of Shelter, the National Campaign
for the Homeless, and commented: 'How effective the
group has been in acting as their representative is
difficult to ascertain, however, since homeless
families play no direct part in the group's
affairs'.(5) He went on to look at the Child
Poverty Action Group, and wrote:

> It is perhaps easier for the Ministries to
> ignore the group as a consequence of the fact
> that it represents no clearly distinct and
> cohesive section of society. Over the years
> ... the group has become increasingly dominated
> by academics. ... the unemployed, the single
> parent and the low wage earner may ... be
> wondering whether any organisations will lead
> their fight for decency and citizenship. (6)

    These organisations will have their answers, as
did some of those in our sample, to cries for
greater consumer involvement in their affairs. As
we have seen in Chapter 4, the clients of CHAR had
been found not to be able to play the part of a
committee member; and FEGH residents were 'too
elderly to do so'. Others claimed that they were in
no way vulnerable to such criticisms: and in any
case consumer involvement is only part of the
process of getting facts right. The point being
made here is that organisations do have a responsibility for providing the highest quality of
information: and this may be the place to say that
statutory agencies with which this was discussed had
a great respect for the knowledge they found in
voluntary organisations with which they had to deal.
    Throughout this and the previous subsection
the common theme has been the need for an openness
to discussion of policy and practice with those who
provide funds in one way or another to make the work
possible. So far as grants are concerned government
departments and voluntary organisations both seem
satisfied with the procedures but we cannot reliably

say very much about other parties. It is true that
our sample did produce some examples of such an
openness with recipients of services but they arose
incidentally, and unfortunately the study could not
be extended to cover this aspect in an adequate way.
There is scope for a whole new study here, of the
extent to which subscribers and consumers
participate in the work: it would be a study, often
at field level, of meetings or less formal occasions
involving recipients of services, or staff providing
them: it would be a study of how information was
obtained and absorbed, and how reliable the
conclusions drawn from it were.

3. To satisfy government agencies set up for the
   purpose: a) that legal or other privileges
   given to charities etc. are not misplaced or
   abused. b) that the organisation is working
   constitutionally, and effectively enough to
   justify the allocation of public funds or
   other resources to it.

Here we are thinking primarily of the Charity
Commission, but also of the Registrar of Friendly
Societies and the Registrar of Companies so far as
a) is concerned, and of the Housing Corporation in
relation to b).
    Charities are 'bound', with certain exceptions,
to register with the Charity Commission. If
registration is refused or withdrawn they will no
longer have the benefits which the law confers upon
charities. Any charity having a permanent endowment
must submit accounts annually to the Commission
unless specially exempted from doing so.
Gladstone's comment on this may be noted in passing:

> It is not easy to see the logic of these
> provisions. Large collecting charities with an
> income of hundreds of thousands of pounds or
> more need not submit accounts so that unless
> the Commissioners require them, the public have
> no right to inspect them; yet endowed charities
> - even those with incomes as low as five or ten
> pounds - must submit their accounts annually.
> In any case, the Commissioners seem not to set
> a high priority to scrutinising accounts
> ...(7)

    Amongst the exceptions to the requirement to
register with the Charity Commission are charitable
housing associations registered under the Industrial

and Provident Societies Acts. They must file their
rules with the Registrar of Friendly Societies and
submit returns to the Registrar on certain matters.
Again the contacts are largely formal. Housing
Associations which wish to obtain grants from
government funds must also register with the Housing
Corporation, which exerts a much more active
supervisory role, requiring accounts in a form
prescribed by the Secretary of State for the
Environment, and undertaking monitoring of the
activities of these associations every two years or
so.

Organisations constituted as companies limited
by guarantee must submit annual accounts, and other
information such as changes in the management
committee, to the Registrar of Companies.

The Charity Commission has the responsibility
to establish charitable status, and no one will
question the importance of charitable organisations
not being used to make profit for those running
them. It also watches over the activities of
charities lest they stray beyond what is regarded as
proper to them. At the present time there is much
questioning of the limitations placed by the
Commission on the definition of charitable activity,
first as to its content and second as to its method.
We have already referred to the NVCO consultation
document, and examples are given in it of areas not
at present regarded as charitable, such as attempts
to help unemployed people, or to promote human
rights. That is the content of charitable activity.
The main issue of contention over method is how far
charities may go in arguing in the political field,
for changes in the law and in administrative
practice.

The NVCO document argues:

It is well established at law that no charity
may seek to advance any party political cause
or other electorally motivated purpose; nor may
a charity's ultimate purposes include securing
or preventing a change in the law or in
administrative policy or practice. We do not
think there is much prospect of removing these
restrictions nor do we believe that to remove
them would necessarily be desirable. But it
is also well established at law that any
charity is free to campaign for or against
changes in the law or its administration as a
means to its ultimate, non-political ends. In
our view this is an important freedom to be

defended.(8)

The document goes on to say that contributing to debates on public policy and administration does not constitute political activity in this context, that this is recognised by the Courts, but that 'the Charity Commissioners in their 1981 Annual Report, issued guidelines on advocacy and campaigning which went considerably beyond the sensible restrictions imposed by the Courts'. This is denied by the Commission.

When asked about their contacts with the Charity Commission the sample organisations all described them as rare or formal, and none of them - hardly surprisingly - had any complaints except perhaps over the slow speed at which the Commission functioned. None of them had been in any way 'vetted' by the Commission in the public interest within recent memory.

This is confirmation that the number of charities 'up against' the Commission over charitable status or indeed on any other matter, is very small, and none of them felt restricted by their terms of trust or charitable status from doing what they wanted to do. It is re-assuring that, for example, no questions were raised with CHAR for its part in getting the Housing (Homeless Persons) Act 1971 on the statute book with all-party support, or in backing a Houses in Multiple Occupation Bill commissioned by CHAR's All-Party Parliamentary Committee: and that FNF takes steps to improve divorce law in the interests of maintaining a child's relationship with both its parents. One would not expect questions to be raised, for guideline no. (iv) of the Commission reads that 'A charity can spend its funds on the promotion of public general legislation only if in doing so it is exercising a power which is ancillary to and in furtherance of its charitable purposes',(9) and CHAR and FNF were clearly exercising a power 'ancillary to and in furtherance of' their main objects. From some of the comments made in the press and in other public discussion on the Charity Commission and its attitude to 'politics', however, one might have expected difficulties and it is pleasing to note that these did not arise. Indeed the experiences of all our sample in the 'social advocacy' role are heartening.

This, it must be added, is not to invalidate the contentions of NCVO quoted above. Inevitably they are concerned with the few organisations which

are pushing at the boundaries of charity law, or
with, as it were, 'nascent' charities unable to form
because of the Commission's attitude to the field in
which they wish to be active. Such charities do not
appear on lists such as our sample was selected
from. Moreover it could be said that our list,
being in the field of 'the welfare state', is of
organisations known to and having some backing from
government departments - a fact which may make
intervention by the Charity Commission less likely.
It could also be said that our sample were less
adventurous than they might have been in pursuing
their causes, and would otherwise not be so happily
placed: of that there is no evidence either way.
    Some reference should now be made to the
Housing Corporation. It has a duty to assure itself
that a housing association receiving public funds of
any sort is functioning suitably. In pursuance of
this it examines accounts and undertakes monitoring
exercises. To quote from The Corporation's Annual
Report for 1982/83:

> ....under Section 124 of the Housing Act 1980,
> (registered associations) are required by law
> to submit their accounts for all accounting
> periods commencing on or after 1st September,
> 1982, within six months of their accounting
> year end. We examine all annual accounts
> received and follow up any queries or causes
> for concern with associations, either
> specifically or through a monitoring visit. We
> also examine annual returns .... to check that
> their committees are properly constituted and
> that there are no unacceptable conflicts of
> interest.(10)

It is interesting, first, to note the requirement of
accounts within six months of the accounting year
end, by comparison with the slowness with which the
accounts of some of our sample are apparently
produced: and, second, to compare the very fact of
the requirement with the Charity Commission's view
quoted earlier 'that the routine collection and
examination of annual accounts does not achieve a
great deal'. It has to be added, however, that
there is an urgency about housing association
accounting because of the extent of government
funding; and that Housing Corporation standard forms
of accounts, relating to bodies all of a similar
kind, though causing difficulties at the time of
writing, will presumably make for more intelligible

analysis.

The Housing Corporation report goes on:

> We have built up .... experienced and skilled
> monitoring staff, ... separate from the day-
> to-day funding of associations. It is our
> policy to visit and monitor, on a regular
> cycle, all registered housing associations
> which have received grants of public money...
> In most cases our monitors have received
> willing co-operation from associations and we
> have been able to take rapid action to help
> them correct any weaknesses in management that
> have been identified.(11)

Only two of our sample were subject to Housing
Corporation procedures, and their comments were made
in 1982. The Housing Corporation has been changing
steadily and by the time this is published the
comments may be less applicable, but it was described by one as a 'difficult master' on finance: both
were of the view that there was too much 'red tape'
and paperwork in the supervisory function, and one
had found that it made demands of the Association at
too short notice. Over the changing of a rule one
of the sample had found 'endless and slow
differences of view' between the Housing Corporation
and the Charity Commission. Both found considerable
variation in their relationship with different
regional offices of the Corporation, and there was
some complaint that the Welsh and Scottish offices
were 'nationalistic and narrow'. RBLHA had found
the Corporation's comments on the need to expand its
membership not realistic, and this aspect has
already been discussed in Chapter 4.

Our conclusions from these contrasting comments
on the Charity Commission and the Housing
Corporation, in the light of other aspects already
discussed, might be:

a)   that the preparation of the accounts of all
     charities should have more attention. There
     should be some degree of standardisation of
     forms. A statement of audited accounts should
     be available within a maximum period of time to
     anyone who asks for them. Some examination
     should be undertaken by the Charity Commission
     or equivalent body. It should be possible to
     learn a good deal from the current relationship
     of Housing Corporation and housing associations
     on this matter.

b) that great sensitivity needs to be achieved in
the supervisory function. The definition of
'charity' may need to be extended, but if, for
this reason or any other such as larger
injections of government funds, there goes with
it an insistence on greater supervision of what
voluntary organisations are doing, there is
also a message to those who monitor. The
experiences of housing associations are a
warning. If the monitoring body is not imbued
with an understanding of the nature of the
voluntary sector it is only too easy for it to
stifle initiative or enterprise by interference, and once that is done the way is open to
some bright politician to conclude that the
sector should be ignored, abolished or taken
over. As we have already indicated, there is a
fine balance between accountability and
independence.

4. In the employment of staff, (paid or voluntary), to provide good terms and conditions of
service, and to encourage their participation
in the process of planning and execution of
activities in accordance with their capacities
and expertise.

This heading is included because it is suggested
that responsibility to staff must come into a list
of aspects of accountability at this point. A study
of the management of voluntary organisations is
perhaps overdue, although some aspects have been
covered recently by Gerard. In his report on a
survey of the organisational aspects of charitable
institutions he concludes that 'as far as management
is concerned, there is disquieting evidence of
complacency and the need both to raise awareness and
improve provision for management education'.(12)
There was some evidence in discussion with the
sample organisations in our own study that management was aware of its need for education, though
this was not a matter specifically raised with the
CEOs who mentioned it.
    Gerard also touched on the specific question of
participation. A good employer has a responsibility
to bring staff into discussions of organisation and
policy, so that they may have assurances about where
the organisation is going, though Gerard observed
that:

Charities engaged in the conservation and

> health fields emerged as predominantly
> hierarchical in style and structure, those in
> community work as predominantly
> participative...Charities which are client-
> centred and those which offer services,
> complementary to statutory provision, are more
> likely to be hierarchical than participative in
> character (p.109).

Gerard went on later to refer to a greater
expression of concern about management problems
being evident in 'new-style' organisations, though
adding:

> Many charities have experienced difficulty in
> reconciling demands for participation and staff
> autonomy with effectiveness and accountability.
> (p.123)
> The organisational problems reported include
> the difficulty of encouraging participation
> without a proliferation of meetings and wasted
> time. (p.137)

The survey on which Gerard was reporting was
carried out in 1978, before the crisis at MIND,
National Association for Mental Health, where the
Director resigned because of a difference of opinion
with the union, ACTSS, over whether the Association
should proceed with a new publication. Here was a
body in the health field, epitomising a clash
between levels of accountability. In the absence of
reports to the contrary it must be assumed that the
Director was acting for his committee and the union
for the staff. However much one favours
participation, and without entering into the affairs
of MIND then and later, there can be no doubt that
the priorities of accountability should mean that
committee decisions should prevail over staff views.
Again, in this study one can only report
impressions received incidentally. These are that
hierarchical structures did predominate, but that
experiments were being made in participation which
were meeting precisely those difficulties described
by Gerard, i.e. of squaring it with accountability
in the other directions which I have placed higher
on the list in this chapter; and of implementing it
without waste of the time of staff members whose
roles and talents lie elsewhere than in endless
meetings.

5. To take account of the views of consumers not
   otherwise represented, and of 'the public'.

By 'consumers not otherwise represented' we mean
people who use the services or facilities provided
by the organisation e.g. as someone obtaining
information from a Citizens' Advice Bureau, but for
whom there is no feedback to the organisation as to
its policy or the quality of the service.
     This is the last outpost of accountability.
'Accountability means responsiveness to comment and
criticism' wrote Hinton and Hyde.(13) '....the
issue of accountability is not merely a question of
controlling malpractice. There is also the much
wider question of public accountability and the
public's right to know how public funds are spent.
For charitable funds are public money....' wrote
Gladstone.(14)
     Gladstone's point about charitable funds being
public money does not impress me in this context,
for it has been taken care of in the registration
and supervision of charities which we have discussed
in Section 3 of this chapter, whether or not we
think that such machinery needs improvement. That a
charity has, like any citizen, a responsibility to
think of its 'neighbour', the community in which it
operates, and the 'colleagues' with which it works,
is a much stronger point: and most citizens are
responsive 'to comment and criticism', in the words
of Hinton and Hyde.
     A national voluntary organisation generally has
more than one 'presence': it has a head office and
its staff there move in a world composed of other
organisations and people doing similar work and
concerned about similar things - the worlds of the
NCVO and the numerous intersecting circles referred
to particularly in Chapter 5. Its willingness to
play its part in those worlds, to be co-operative
and considerate with others, is one aspect of being
responsive.
     There is also the local 'presence'. Many of
those in our sample were, for example, responsible
for residential homes or other establishments, and
these must play their part in the local community.
As the NFHA has stated in respect of its member
associations:

     .....We believe that....housing associations
     frequently account directly and personally for
     their actions to the communities in which they
     work, in ways that pure public bodies would

find difficult.(15)

This may, one hopes, be applied equally well to any voluntary establishment.

Having said this, one must however go on to warn that this sense of accountability must have its limits. If voluntary organisations fall over backwards to be responsive to every local pressure they will lose all sense of real identity. The impression is sometimes given that on the score of accountability any local busybody should have a right to say what the organisation should be doing. Specialist associations exist to adopt policies within their specialised interests: no local councillor has a right to say, even if they all do, that an advantage should be given to someone in his district over someone from outside; because an organisation is based in a particular community, that community has no right to say who is to be housed on its estate which happens to be there too. The national voluntary organisation must insist that its priorities, e.g. in the care of the elderly or the housing of the disabled, must come first.

Our study did not extend to an examination of work and relationships at local level, so it cannot produce evidence of what goes on there. This, fifth, section on accountability is therefore a statement of precept rather than of practice. It completes this chapter on accountability in which it has been suggested that priorities are

1. The terms of trust and the members.
2. Those who provide the funds.
3. Clients or consumers.
4. Government 'watch-dogs'.
5. Staff.
6. Public.

All discussion of this difficult subject points to our need to realise that accountability is not homogeneous, that to observe it we must be selective, and that this may sometimes involve us in difficult decisions. Until we have established our priorities discussion will continue to be affected too much by changes of political fashion.

REFERENCES

1.   See Ashworth, Herbert. The Building Society Story. Franey, London, 1980.

2. NCVO. Charity Law: a case for change? 1983.
3. Best, Richard. The Government and the
        Voluntary Sector. Unpublished memorandum.
        National Federation of Housing Associa-
        tions, 1979.
4. Holland, P. and Fallon, M. The Quango
        Explosion. Conservative Political Centre,
        1978.
5. Seyd, Patrick. 'Shelter: the National Campaign
        for the Homeless', article in Political
        Quarterly, Vol. 46, pp.418 - 431. 1975.
6. Seyd, Patrick. 'The Child Poverty Action
        Group', article in Political Quarterly,
        Vol.47, pp.189 - 202. 1976. (pp.199 & 200)
7. Gladstone, Francis. Charity, Law and Social
        Justice. Bedford Square Press, London,
        1982.
8. Op. cit.
9. Report of the Charity Commissioners for England
        and Wales for the year 1981, (p.21).
        H.M.S.O., 1982.
10. The Housing Corporation Report 1982/83, (p.11).
11. Op. cit.
12. Gerard, David. Charities in Britain: conserv-
        atism or change? Bedford Square Press,
        London, 1983.
13. Hinton, N. and Hyde, M. 'The voluntary sector
        in a remodelled Welfare State', article in
        The Year Book of Social Policy 1980 - 81.
        Routledge and Kegan Paul, London.
14. Op. cit.
15. Housing Associations: Philosophy and Accounta-
        bility. A statement of Policy from the
        National Federation of Housing Associa-
        tions. 1983.

Chapter 7

FUTURE PROSPECTS

> There can be no question of returning to the
> grim conditions of the nineteenth century.
> Attempts to move beyond the Welfare State must
> preserve and build on its achievements while
> seeking to accomplish them in more effective
> ways.
>
> - NCVO in <u>Beyond</u> <u>the</u> <u>Welfare</u> <u>State</u>?

National voluntary organisations (nvos) play a
lively and significant part in contemporary social
welfare. Table 2.2 shows that well over half the
150 organisations from which our sample was taken
were formed since the Second World War. The number
of organisations against the years 1900 - 1919 would
have to be multiplied by five, and those of the
inter-war years trebled, to achieve the same rate of
formation per annum as the period 1946 onwards. It
is also of interest to see that even since 1970 the
rate has been over two per annum, the same as for
1946 - 1969. Even allowing for those formed earlier
which are now defunct, it seems indisputable that
the latter part of the 19th Century produced a crop
of very hardy organisations in this field, and that
so far the second half of the 20th Century is doing
the same. The figures are a convincing answer to
the once-made assumption that with the welfare state
voluntary bodies would fade away.
     It is open to argument whether this steady
increase in numbers is due to dissatisfaction with
the basic welfare state, or to a flowering and
refinement of the provisions and ideas which the
latter has produced. What is not open to argument
is that it epitomises extensive social concern of
the very kind that brought the welfare state into
existence, a concern which all parties will surely
agree must be fostered and built on. In what
directions is it likely, or is it desirable, that
further development will or should go? This final
chapter will largely be devoted to future
prospects, but first it may be helpful to reiterate
where our earlier chapters have taken us.

Future Prospects

THE PRESENT

Our analysis has shown that nvos are of a wide
variety of size, with annual incomes in our sample
varying between £1,000 and £6m, and a median of
£375,000. Though as we have seen in Chapter 2, our
sample does not include the very wealthiest measured
by total income, it is perhaps instructive to
compare the voluntary scale of activity with that of
statutory agencies in relevant fields. Local
authority Social Service Departments' expenditures
in 1982/3 ranged between just below £10 million to
over £70 million, with a median of £20 million for
County Councils and over £12 million for Metropolitan Districts. District Health Authorities ranged
between just less than £10 million and over £80
million, with a median of £43 million. A survey by
the Charities Aid Foundation showed that only seven
charities in the population of 150 from which our
sample was taken had total incomes of more than
£12m, of which four exceeded £20m, the largest of
all being Dr. Barnardos' at £29,887,000.(1) Thus we
may see that very few nvos operate on the scale of a
Metropolitan District SSD, and the average annual
expenditure is less than 1% that of a District
Health Authority.
     Nvos do a variety of things and we identified
examples of those for which they seem to be
particularly well suited. In personal services
these included residential care, adoption, special
housing, and holidays. There were a number of
arguments for these being organised by a national
body - ability to provide particular expertise;
virtues of not too small an organisation; clientele
being drawn from the country as a whole: the
service concerned being essentially a country-wide
service, and so on. That there are also arguments
for some of them to be provided on a local basis is
undeniable, but for a few the specialist concern of
the nvo makes the case for centralised provision
very much stronger. FEGH for the gentlefolk; MHCAA
for people with a particular kind of religious
faith; MHA for those wishing to live in the historic
houses the Association exists to preserve; NGEC to
advise the gypsies; and RBLHA to house retired ex-
service people. These examples bring out clearly
one of the predominant features of many voluntary
organisations, that they are specialised and that
their motive power springs from this fact.
     Another feature which has always been
emphasised ad nauseam by protagonists of the

153

voluntary sector, that it undertakes pioneering work, is shown by our study not to be a hollow claim. The part played by RADAR in the establishment of Motability; the Volunteer Stroke Schemes of CHSA; schemes for housing with associated care being tried by JGAD; the school and medical service for pregnant schoolgirls run by MHCAA; are recent examples thrown up by our study, and there are various ideas for new experiments developing. Some of these are not appropriate in the long run for extensive provision by nvos: Volunteer Stroke Schemes, for example, are given provisional and administrative backing for three years and intended then to be taken over by local statutory or voluntary bodies. Others may suitably become a national service - as Motability, started by RADAR but now independent, has shown.

The study has brought out clearly how important is the provision by nvos of background services - publications, special expertise, courses and conferences, library facilities. The advice and information function is a substantial one, whether for clients or clients' helpers, or for local bodies undertaking various activities. 'Advice and information' is distinguished from casework, normally an essentially local function, though CCE indicates that casework involving a very particular knowledge - in this case of the kinds and qualities of homes for the elderly - may usefully be more centralised. Library facilities, perhaps a slightly more academic background service, were found in only five service organisations though they were of good standard in the study-type of nvo which HCT represents, and in the well-established pressure groups like CHAR and NAWCH.

'Social advocacy' is shown to be a function not restricted to pressure groups, and pressure groups are not always restricted to social advocacy, which we have seen may be in the form of publications, submissions to committees of enquiry or to government departments, parliamentary activity or press campaigns. Although we saw that research and intelligence played too small a part in the work of all our sample, and there was notably little study of consumer views, pressure groups are otherwise well informed, - and it was interesting to find that this was recognised by nearly all of the government and local government spokesmen I saw, whose respect for them in this connection was evident. This could not always be said of the service organisations, a few of whom were clearly not well-informed about the wider context of their work.

The role of the intermediary body was seen to be important. Even some of our sample organisations, which all had some claims to be national in scope, depended for their access to and influence on government on the intermediary body or bodies to which they were affiliated. The 'case history' of NCVCCO which we undertook showed that a quite small organisation can do valuable work of this sort, and it was apparent that many intermediary bodies are of the nature of 'one man and a dog', though others, such as RADAR, count the intermediary role as part of, if not ancillary to, several other roles for which the organisation exists and they are therefore much larger.

As to the quality of the work of the nvos we examined, the conclusions were that they were governed by well-qualified committees, though we made various suggestions for improvement of their composition and functioning; and well served by their staff. Even the senior civil servant who wondered about the professional efficiency and ability of such staff spoke of their being '120% in terms of commitment'. Efficiency was not measurable in this study, except where the lack of it was forced upon one by people who did not answer letters or 'phone back when they said they would - these did exist, but then so they do elsewhere. Amongst some of the CEOs interviewed there was concern at the organisation's inability to monitor its performance, and this applied not only to financial aspects, on which we have made critical comments. We can support the findings of the Gallup study of charitable institutions written up by Gerard: 'three-quarters of the organisations sampled agreed with the statement that: 'Some form of (performance) appraisal should be developed for the benefit of both those running the organisations and the general public'.'(2)

There was constant reiteration too from the organisations seen in our study that there was no way of knowing what part their representations on behalf of particular policies had played in their ultimate adoption. We discussed this in Chapter 5 and concluded that there was some reason to think that well-presented arguments did have their effect, even though it remained unacknowledged, but there is perhaps a good case for more careful assessment, if not research, on what ways are most effective. For the moment one may comment that it is a matter for amazement and admiration that so many go on

espousing their causes with little but faith to
inspire them. We return to one aspect of this
matter, parliamentary activity, later in this
chapter.

Towards the end of 1983 a little booklet
published by NCVO, Government Grants, had more
publicity than it might reasonably have expected.
Designed as a guide to voluntary organisations
wishing to apply for government funds, it included
as an introduction a table of Central Government
Grants to Voluntary Organisations 1979/80 - 1982/83.
This showed an increase in grants from most
government departments, in cash terms, and the four
departments with which this study has been mostly
concerned were cited as follows:

Department	1979/80 £000	1982/83 £000	% increase /decrease
DES	12,400	11,175	- 10%
DoE (direct grants)	679	976	+ 44%
DHSS	10,090	15,462	+ 53%
Home Office	10,875	16,514	+ 52%

Publicity concentrated on this table, and The Times
wrote of the 'noteworthy increase in the subventions
from central government to voluntary and charitable
bodies in the four years since Mrs. Thatcher took
office'; but went on to talk of the 'case for
pruning the ever-lengthening list of interest groups
knocking, apparently successfuly, on Whitehall
doors'.(3) We shall discuss later in this chapter,
what are the merits and demerits of voluntary
organisations taking a larger proportion of public
funds and playing a larger part in public welfare,
but for now it needs to be said that our study
showed 12 organisations getting no grants at all for
general work, and only 3 of these getting grants for
specific purposes. It comes out loud and clear from
our study that even amongst nvos half of them are
getting on with doing their own job of work as best
they can with the funds they can raise, and do not
get - and may not want - government support.

Another feature of our conclusions was that
being a pressure group did not preclude receipt of
government grant: we saw that CHAR and NAWCH did
particularly well. The Times saw this aspect too,

referring to money which 'undoubtedly goes to charitable bodies with an avowedly political intent (such as the Child Poverty Action Group) and to organisations at cross-purposes with the government's social policy' - but went on, to its credit, to add that 'of course, such pluralism is a welcome index of political maturity.'(4)

The NVCO booklet just referred to provides a useful account of present support from central government, and brings out clearly how much of that support is for short-term work of one kind or another. The DHSS, for example, has aims such as getting mentally handicapped children back into the community, providiing opportunities for the unemployed to do voluntary work, and instigating new initiatives e.g. on intermediate treatment, or day care for the under-fives: the often vaunted grants for general work play a relatively small part.

Longer-term support may be seen at the DES where grants appear mainly to be devoted to recurrent work by voluntary youth organisations and those providing adult education: these fields were supported long before the present or even previous governments were in office. The Home Office like-wise supports marriage guidance work, and rehabili-tation and after-care of offenders, and the DoE has a small amount available for housing advice which is national in scope or innovative in nature, for organisations concerned with homelessness.

Short-term or not, and leaving housing aside, grants in three of the four departments have increased in cash terms during the last three years, as the table shows. Increases, however, even of 50% have to be seen in the context of inflation over the same period of 35 - 40%, and if we take that in the context of the relatively small part which the sector plays, by comparison with the statutory, it will be seen that in financial terms there is no obvious government move significantly to change the balance of provision between statutory and voluntary. Yet government spokesmen continue to make it plain that they will, to quote one of them recently, 'be looking to the voluntary sector to complement and supplement public provision,'(5) and this implies an expanding role.

There was no opportunity to discuss with nvos how they would view a request to expand their work substantially; and some would have regarded it as a rather meaningless exercise without their knowing first the extent of expansion proposed, the directions in which it was requested, whether they

would get financial backing from government funds
and if so for how long and on what terms, to mention
just the most obvious questions that would arise.
That nvos were largely in favour of the continued
existence of the voluntary sector might be expected
- the main reasons given being the quality of work
some were able to achieve, the view that certain
work was essentially or desirably a voluntary
organisation's function, the importance of choice
being available to the client/consumer, and the
valuable influences which the voluntary and
statutory bring to bear on each other. These
arguments were however in no cases but the housing
associations used to urge that the voluntary sector
be given greater support to achieve a much larger
role. Nvos felt that their current role was
significant even though very modest in size.

Amongst the civil servants there was no
unanimity on this question. On the one hand was the
view that the present balance was good, roles were
different and should remain so: on the other that
the potential for voluntary organisations was
'enormous', limited only by money and the ability of
head office staff to keep control of the expansion.
There was also an expression of apprehension, as it
were on behalf of the voluntary sector, of a danger
of it becoming an agent of government, when it could
lose its entity and its vigour and therefore perhaps
all that makes it worthwhile.

A HYPOTHETICAL FUTURE

It may be worthwhile to take this matter a little
further, and to look at what potentialities our
sample reveals for a substantial hand-over of
responsibilities from state to voluntary
organisations. Suppose that the government,
extending its policy of privatisation of industry,
decided to 'voluntarise' some of the social
services: this might for example include the
transfer of all residential care from local
authorities to the voluntary sector. What
organisations are available to take this on?

First there is the Church Army, experienced in
this field: but its main concern is 'mission', and
its social welfare work is secondary to it. Is an
irreligious, non-proselytizing, electorate going to
be happy about this? Perhaps it will, if a whole
lot of others are brought in too, as a counter-
balance. Whether CA itself would wish to extend,
perhaps weakening its mission in the process, is

another matter, and one which would apply too to
MHCAA, which promotes an evangelical faith accepted
by relatively few in Britain today.

Then there is FEGH - unlikely one would think
to wish to extend its work to other than
'gentlefolk', though perhaps willing to extend its
definition of the word. Would this be a suitable
channel into which to divert the responsibilities of
the National Assistance Acts? Again, could the
answer be 'yes' if there were numerous others
providing accommodation for a variety of kinds of
people, like John Groom's or Shaftesbury Homes in
our sample?

In a policy of voluntarising public housing
there would be similar questions to answer. RBLHA
could undoubtedly provide a great deal more
sheltered accommodation for the elderly, but would
it wish to house other than ex-service people, and
if not how far is the state justified in expanding
privileged access to such housing to ex-service
people? Is this all right if the relatively few
others doing the same job but without special
criteria, Hanover and Anchor and Abbeyfield, are
also given support?

One might note in passing that both FEGH and
RBLHA are examples of bodies which may find their
clientele - gentlefolk and ex-service people -
declining in numbers. Are they in the long run to
widen their clientele, or give a distorted service
to the fewer clients available e.g. sheltered
housing to people who do not need it, or extra
luxury to fewer gentlepeople?

The sample indicates that there are
organisations getting on with a job not at present
seen as a welfare state function at all,
organisations which therefore would not presumably
be considered for a new role. These include CCE
and MHA, as well as the pressure groups. Others
currently aim to provide back-up for local bodies
which have sprung up to meet a need particular to a
locality - e.g. SHA or WEA: there is no concept of
a uniform national service of hostels for those in
deprived circumstances, or particular courses in
further education, ready to be extended or taken
over by nvos.

We find ourselves therefore with a relatively
few nvos on the face of it poised to have a dual
role with statutory agencies: BDA, with schemes
for the deaf; CHSA, with volunteer stroke schemes;
RADAR for the handicapped; are the three about which
we have expressed no reservation above. What would

be required to facilitate the expansion we have
envisaged?

Inevitably the first answer is funds. It
varies according to what the service is, but most
obviously residential care requires substantial
capital funds for bricks and mortar alone: there is
no access to public funds, whether by grant or loan,
for this at present. It contrasts with the situation
in housing, in which housing associations may obtain
support up to nearly 100% of the cost of their
schemes via the Housing Corporation or local
authorities, - though in practice support is
decreasingly available at the moment. Nvos which
provide residential care find it almost impossible
to raise the large funds necessary to build new
homes.

Other services may require less funds.
Holidays, for example, should largely pay for
themselves, and may very suitably be undertaken by
nvos. Personal social services or social work
depend very much on local organisations, asking only
for back-up by nvos which may not be costly. Other
schemes fall midway between. In 1983 for example,
Devon SSD planned a network of six IT units in co-
operation with the National Children's Home: each
unit will have two full-time NCH staff supported by
about a dozen volunteers, an educational
psychologist and part-time clerical help: the
outgoings were to be in the nature of revenue
expenditure rather than capital, and -like most of
the other services referred to in this paragraph-
related to local, not central, government funding.

This takes us to another question; what could
be the role of local government in funding
comprehensive services provided by, or at least the
responsibility of, national voluntary organisations?
In the conditions prevailing in 1984 it is difficult
to imagine central government making funds available
to local authorities adequate for the support of
voluntary organisations providing services hitherto
undertaken by those authorities themselves. It is
equally difficult to imagine local authorities being
encouraged or even permitted to raise their own
funds for the purpose. Even with an enormous shift
of attitudes towards local authorities, it is
certain that any service dependent on their subsidies would be very patchy in geographical terms.

A substantial increase in statutory funding is
therefore likely to mean an increase in central
government funding, and this is bound to mean a more
extensive interest by government in what the

organisations receiving it are doing and how they
are doing it. As we have seen in Chapter 6 this is
not always to the liking of such organisations:
examination of accounts and of whether committees
are properly constituted are obvious necessities,
but if a body like the Housing Corporation is set up
specially to provide supervision there seems to be a
danger of it becoming 'trigger-happy' in its criticisms of the voluntary organisations' functions. We
have, for example, noted demands to bring others
into membership which are based on a misunderstand-
ing of the nature of the organisation: and perhaps
at the other end of the scale of importance, the
imposition of paperwork which a short-staffed
voluntary body finds irksome. If a larger voluntary
sector role were to be accompanied by quango supervision, care would be needed to ensure that it was a
very understanding supervision if the spirit of
voluntary effort was not to be damped down.

Another implication of more extensive government funding could be that there would be several
voluntary organisations being funded in the same
field, and this would mean that the responsibility
for 'holding the ring' would be the greater. Though
nvos accept that where government holds the funds it
has a right to say to what organisations those funds
shall go, nvos do expect to see equity in the
process. Where there is an intermediary body the
value of government using the knowledge of the field
that body should have would be all the more
important. Even this present small study, of
circumstances in which government funding is not
enormous, threw up one example of a major nvo
apparently missing substantial grant aid through an
oversight on the part of the government department
responsible.

So far in our discussion the assumption has
been made that statutory funds would be diverted to
nvos to facilitate the growth of the latter. This
may not be how those who wish to recast our welfare
society would see it. The Secretary of State for
Social Services has warned us 'that over the next
few years (public) resources are going to be very
tight indeed'(6) and perhaps the aim is cherished of
a return to funds being raised for many of these
services from public subscriptions or by a market
approach being made in many cases.

Public subscription, i.e. amounts raised from
fund-raising and donations (including legacies) in
1980 comprised 12.9% of the income of the sample of
charities quoted by the Charities Aid Foundation.(7)

The Foundation also indicated that total voluntary income as shown by an 'ad hoc selection of forty charities' increased in 1983 by 12% compared with 1982. The Foundation adds:

> The element of fund-raising presently appearing to lack financial impact is, not perhaps surprisingly in view of its comparatively late arrival on the scene, the pay roll deduction. Only three of the bigger and two of the smaller charities out of the twenty-eight participating charities returning figures under this heading, yet it is predictably one of the future's most promising and easily organised source of revenue.(8)

Some have expressed the view that as the state withdraws so company giving will increase. The CAF figures for the top two hundred Corporate Donors for the years 1979-83 shows little evidence of this. Their donations rose, in 1981-2 prices, from £30.8m in 1978-9 to £31.1m in 1981-2.

Apart from the pay roll deduction an increase in fund-raising and donations must therefore presumably depend upon even more effective appeals. One shudders at the thought in the light of the aggressive appeal activities now in vogue, abusing as they do the susceptibilities of many recipients with their bullying and blackmailing: and if any reader should consider these to be strong words let him look at Appendix J. Certainly there is good reason for a code of conduct to be accepted in this field. In general however, the impression one has is that though voluntary giving may increase gradually in real terms, it cannot be expected to be of such magnitude that it would enable the voluntary sector to take on a different role.

The market approach requires that more of the services being provided by nvos be charged for. At present the income from 'fees and subscriptions' (unfortunately not separated) is shown by CAF to comprise 42.7% of total income, so a relatively slight percentage increase would be quite significant. There are instances in which an increase in subscriptions could apparently be very reasonably expected. In our sample, BDA's annual subscription of 10p is ludicrous, stemming back as it must to days when any group for which a just cause had been promoted was assumed de facto to be poor. This may be true of the homeless and rootless, but does it apply to the deaf?

It must be made clear that the CAF figures for
fees are <u>gross</u>, and do not even imply that they
cover costs, let alone make a surplus for general
funds. Fees, for services rendered to individuals,
are in many cases negotiated with local authorities,
and are unlikely to be over-generous. Our sample
showed little income from fees or charges, except in
some cases for conferences and sales of
publications, but their figures were <u>net</u>.
Some organisations (not in our sample) have had
to consider asking for fees when in the past their
services had been free to all. The London Marriage
Guidance Council was reported in 1983 as being in
acute financial difficulties due to a fall in local
authority grants (i.e. general subsidies); to quote
its Annual Report, 'If our grants do not hold up
then the alternatives are depressing. We could
instigate a minimum charge or we could go in for
some kind of means testing to determine each
client's fee'. It was maintained that this would
discourage poorer people from using the service and
the report concluded: 'We do not intend to let
ourselves be driven into the private sector by
charging realistic fees and we are determined to
continue to offer help where it is needed, rather
than where it pays off'.
This example shows vividly, first just how
much the voluntary sector has hitherto been
universalist in its approach, and second how it has
to face all the same arguments for and against
selectivity as the state if it finds itself eager to
give a much needed service in adverse financial
circumstances. The answer of many organisations, as
our sample has shown, is to provide free services to
the extent that funds permit: quantity, frequency,
accessibility, quality, may suffer, but charges are
not made. That there are arguments for selective
charges is I suspect not always given enough
consideration, but no amount of consideration is
likely to make it possible for the voluntary sector
to take a comprehensive service over from the
statutory on the basis of charging fees.
We return now to the question posed on page 160
as to what would be required to facilitate an
expansion of nvos to enable them to play a major
part with the state in the provision of public
services. Funds are basic, and we have discussed
them briefly. Inevitably the next thing required
would be more extensive organisation. It is
generally agreed that work that depends on local
spontaneity is patchy, and though the so-called

universal services of the welfare state are much
more patchy than sometimes admitted, a serious
attempt at equity must be made, and this means
vigorous promotional activity by a central or
regional organisation. This would almost certainly
lead to nvos having a greatly increased bureaucratic
structure: the theoretical alternative of a large
number of small national organisations is unlikely
to be found in practice - though to point to a
possible exception, DES is reported even now to be
making grants to 60 national voluntary youth
organisations.(9) The sort of structure more likely
to be needed is illustrated by RBLHA, which in 1982
had eight regional offices, and 111 full-time staff
apart from wardens of housing schemes. Each scheme
had its own house committee. A similar development
was seen in the organisations of the other nvos in
this field, Hanover and Anchor Housing Associations.
Though not large by comparison with big commercial
firms, they are approaching the point when
management problems arise, and the very nature of
voluntary effort may change.

The general impression given by visits to the
nvos in our sample, though it was not put into words
by those who were interviewed, was of a belief in a
certain intimacy of organisation. Some known to the
author certainly believe that it is good to remain
relatively small, to retain a face-to-face
relationship within the staff. One virtue still of
many voluntary bodies is a relative absence of the
we-they, employees - management, situation; another
is the near unity of staff and management on the
aims of the organisation; if unionization does not
destroy this, and there is still hope that it will
not, size might, and with any prospect of an nvo
growing to provide a substantial 'infrastructure'
service the questions would have to be asked: Would
it be long before it became indistinguishable in
type and quality of service from a statutory body?
Could it maintain the specialised and more personal
service for which it has been customary to look to
voluntary organisations? Will it be able to
maintain anything of a crusading independent social
advocacy role that it may have had hitherto? Will
it any longer be regarded as unbiassed in its
provision of background advice and information for
local oranisations if it is closely associated with,
if not funded by, the state? Will it continue to
get support and service of the same quantity and
quality from voluntary workers and committee
members?

If the answer is 'no' to many of these
questions, then to extend nvo work in the ways we
have discussed would mean a conscious decision to
create a different kind of nvo, one of the kind that
is found in Holland, where the voluntary sector is
the agent of the state in the provision of social
services. According to Brenton,(10)in the
Netherlands, government subsidies to voluntary
agencies have risen to nearly one hundred per cent
of costs. The model which is developing is 'the
incorporated model', where agencies enter into a
closer relationship with the state financially, and
become quasi-public services in many respects. The
Dutch government is now attaching more conditions to
the receipt of subsidies - quality control relating
to staff establishments, training, hours worked,
salary rates etc. Some might say that these
organisations sound suspiciously like quangos, and
who in GB is going to argue in favour of such a
proposal?
    The present government has supposedly set
itself against quangos, yet if it wished to adopt
extensive voluntarisation as an ideological move it
would have to face the paradox that very similar
bodies may be required to achieve it. For our part
it seems clear that there are no arguments except
the ideological for development of this kind.
Certainly arguments based on the values of pluralism
do not apply to it.

A MORE PROBABLE FUTURE

The hypothetical future we have just discussed for
service organisations is not a likely one. No one
that I met who was really knowledgeable, whether in
politics, govermment or the voluntary sector,
seriously argued for it. For social advocacy
functions it has of course no relevance.
    This is not to say that there will not be some
nvos who may be willing to take the Dutch road, or
that there is not more scope for voluntary-statutory
cooperation; especially in new fields, specialised
fields, non-universalist provision where size is
limited, and the flexibility and informality which
is recognised to be a voluntary body's attribute can
get things going with relatively small money. It is
important to keep it that way and not to push the
nvo down the bureaucratic or narrow professional
roads. As one civil servant put it: 'Bureaucracy
comes from having to be consistent, which voluntary
organisations don't have to be' - they can undertake

some 'one-off' service and not worry about setting a precedent.

A more probable future for nvos will be that they will be encouraged, by government grants and in other ways, to be active in particular fields. The initiative may come from a government department, as with the DHSS on intermediate treatment or on services for the under-fives. Sometimes the reason may be that it is in government's interests that otherwise unpopular groups, such as delinquents and prisoners, are seen to have some support in society, to justify the direct action which the government sees it necessary to take. Whatever the reason for it, support will usually be in the nature of encouraging small scale experimental and rarely universal activity. If this is so it is a future which the voluntary movement should welcome.

It is on the way to the future which was advocated by Gladstone in his Voluntary Action in a Changing World. 'Welfare pluralism', an 'evolutionary rather than revolutionary ...... demonopolising strategy ...... would hinge on a steadily increasing role for voluntary action';

> ...it would also include elements of decentralisation (more local involvement in decision-making), de-standardisation (more support for innovative and experimental programmes) and de-professionalisation (more emphasis on informal care and self-help together with a shift to prevention and the horizontal integration of services). In such a scenario the role of the Government gradually becomes the upholding of equity in resource allocation, the enforcement of minimum standards, the fostering of more pluralistic legislation and the use of fiscal and regulatory law both for income maintenance and to reinforce a preventive approach.(11)

A discussion paper later issued by NCVO gave support to Gladstone: '....we would argue that a pluralist approach to the provision of some, indeed many, welfare services can provide the most prom-ising strategy for the future'.(12) Whether the government of 1984, or in the future, would go as far as Gladstone in fostering pluralism one cannot say: indeed it is not clear how far he would him-self want to go; suffice it to say that the present gentle moves in that direction can be welcomed.

The initiative, however, will not rest solely

or even largely with the statutory sector, and it is
certainly important that nvos do not become dependent for their existence on relatively large statutory funds from one source, whether for agency or
general work.

It must be remembered that our focus is on
national voluntary organisations, many of which are
not able to call on local government fees or grants.
Where they are the strength of a multiplicity of
sources of income may be apparent. For example, in
the RNIB, as the Director-General wrote in a
personal communication to the author: 'Our one-
third income from fees and charges comes from 124
different local authorities and may come from three
different departments (SSD, LEA, and libraries):
this gives us independence, not dependence or
interference'.

The virtue of nvos must be an ability to remain
independent: to harness the energies of people who
want to give help for a particular cause, and to
remain single minded in their approach, with a
vision unclouded by financial or party-political
limitations. Wherever dependence on public funds
becomes very extensive, as the housing association
movement demonstrates, it becomes regarded as
'public sector', and treated accordingly by the
government of the day whether it be on cuts in
public expenditure, or in Treasury red tape in
accounting for use of funds: the voluntary sector
must avoid this, for in truth it is a different
creature altogether from both the public and the
private sectors, and it must shout this out and live
accordingly.

This applies even more to pressure groups. One
cannot but be impressed by the 'political maturity'
which permits government grants to bodies which bite
the hand which feeds them. No doubt it is not
always the same type of political maturity as we
imagine: the politician or administrator may well
see something in having things both ways - able
officially to appear to have one view whilst
discreetly planting or supporting pressure for
another, which can at some point be graciously
'accepted': or able to use the voluntary
organisation to put pressure on local authorities or
health authorities when government itself cannot, or
does not wish to do so. Long may this continue, but
such pressure groups (and there are only some to
which it applies) must also beware lest at some
point the 'mature' hand ceases to feed them.

Throughout the discussion so far, voluntary-statutory relationship has appeared to be on a par with 'Man proposes God disposes'. We concluded at the end of Chapter 5 that there was little joint planning or consultation between nvos and government departments. It is interesting to have some confirmation of this, as this chapter was being completed, from quite another viewpoint. The Organisational Analysis Research Unit of the University of Bradford Management Centre have been undertaking research into the voluntary sector. A paper written in March 1984 concludes that there are now a multitude of national associations, headed by the NCVO, 'which co-ordinate and control the activities of voluntary organisations and also liaise with central government' (what in our terminology would be named 'intermediary'): but that there is not real co-operation between state and voluntary sector because the state retains ultimate control. The paper cites three ways in which this is exerted.

1) The power of the Charity Commission to decide between what activities are charitable and what are not, and the concomitant desire of the Commission to preserve the status quo
2) A pressure to persuade voluntary organisations to offer services along existing lines of those performed by many state agencies and not to act as an alternative source
3) A pressure to persuade voluntary organisations to operate along the lines of state bureaucracies.

'The net result', says the paper, is 'a stifling of the potential contribution of the voluntary sector to the mixed economy'.(13)

The conclusions of our own work would not fully support the Bradford Unit's assessments, on the one hand, of the power wielded by the national (intermediary) associations, nor, on the other, of the effect of the Charity Commission and other government pressures: but our two viewpoints unite in the conclusion that there is a need for more effective consultation on policy between nvos and government departments. If the former are to have a gradually increasing service role, if their knowledge is respected and their views on policy well thought out, it is time for better, and perhaps more equal, opportunities for thinking together to

be created. Even in industry, where confrontation
more often hits the headlines than co-operation, and
is certainly more rife than in social welfare, there
is the National Economic Development Council and,
perhaps more important because more practically
effective, the 'little Neddies', the 50 or more
working parties covering sectors of manufacturing
and service industry. Is there not an argument for
similar bodies to be established for sectors of
social welfare?

In an article in The Times on the occasion of
NEDC's 21st anniversary, Keith Middlemas wrote:

> ...it is the only British organisation which is
> dedicated wholly to the pursuit of beneficial
> change in a relatively non-political
> quantifiable way.
> By enunciating clearly what industry
> needs, on the basis of independent analysis, it
> acts as a guardian of the public interest in
> industry without actually becoming a lobby for
> industry or a representative like CBI or TUC.
> It presents an accurate, disaggregated picture
> of industries and their current problems, not
> filtered by ideology or civil servants' natural
> tendency to systematize.(14)

Substitute 'social welfare' for 'industry' and it
could be a description of what is now required.
There would be little neddies for maternity, the
under-fives, disablement, the elderly, poverty,
higher education etc. composed of representatives of
government departments; major nvos and particularly
intermediary bodies for the sectors concerned; local
and/or health authorities; the private sector; the
trade unions. For people who do to meet people who
plan; for people who spend to meet people who pay;
for people who provide or could provide information,
to meet people who would like to use it; there can
be nothing but good arise from such an opportunity.

I am not advocating an executive role for such
bodies, and I am not unaware that advisory bodies
are sometimes a godsend to the Minister or civil
servant who wishes to evade action or decision or
admission of his own views. Nor am I unaware of the
restriction which being party to such bodies would
place on the social advocacy organisation: I would
argue that behind-the-scenes advocacy could be more
effective in some respects, and that headlines
advocacy would still not be inhibited but should be
more knowledgeable and responsible as a result of

participation in the bodies suggested.

Nvos may deserve a larger part in planning policy than they have been given, but they have failed it seems to play the part they could in the parliamentary process. In discussions with members of the four main parties it was made abundantly clear that contacts between the parties and nvos are at best a matter of chance (people who happen to be members of both party and nvo), and at worst, and more commonly, non-existent. If nvos are consulted at all it is more likely to be after a policy has been drafted than before: speeches made in Parliament may take account of nvo views, but are more likely to be the result of a hasty telephone call to an unknown information officer than of a sustained personal acquaintance with the cause. We have seen in Chapter 3 that five of our sample mentioned parliamentary activity, and three of these saw it as largely a matter of working through an all-party group, but this clearly has its limitations. Though some nvos do cultivate individual parliamentary contacts, and know the detail of parliamentary processes and how they can best be used, most of them do not; if they make efforts to get their views known they may waste their time by doing so at the wrong moment and to the wrong persons; when they could make useful efforts they fail to do so. Certainly a more effective role in the future could be secured by nvos taking trouble to find out how each party works, and how therefore the nvo's knowledge and views could be transmitted to it; and how the parliamentary process works and could be used either for promoting a cause or legislative change necessary to a cause. The fact that there is a steady increase in the numbers of lobbyists for social welfare causes in Parliament shows that there is a growing appreciation of this.

We have been thinking hitherto about the national scene. There is also much scope for improvement of the effectiveness of nvos at local level. Where there are local groups or branches of a national organisation it may be largely a matter of support and encouragement of such bodies, by the national headquarters, to establish good co-operation with, or representation to, the local statutory organisations in the field: but as we saw in Chapter 4 only four of the sample had branches or the equivalent, and two of these (CHAR and NAWCH) are pressure groups, leaving BDA and WEA among service organisations. Some nvos have field officers and Table 4.2 set out other local

activitities, but overall it is clear that contacts
with local authorities at anything approaching
policy level are very limited if they exist at all.
    This puts a pointed emphasis on a fact which
became very plain in all my discussions with such
bodies as local authority associations and the
National Association of Health Authorities: it is
that contacts between national voluntary
organisations and local statutory bodies are almost
non-existent. Whereas local voluntary bodies quite
often get financial support from central government,
the other 'channel' of local-central is not open.
There are exceptions, and one has been quoted
earlier in this chapter (page 160), the Devonshire
CC - National Children's Home co-operation over IT
units, but in the main there is no way in which
either nvo or local authority can know of an
openness on the part of the other to such opportunities for co-operation.
    Nor is it only a question of co-operation on
practical schemes. Often a pressure group wishes to
exert influence on local government practices: but
how often does it not assume that the best way to do
so is via central government? It is no doubt easier
that way, and Patrick Jenkin, Secretary of State for
the Environment, has recently invited an assumption
that it is the best way, by making clear his view
that Britain's is a unitary state and local
government must obey central dictates. Whilst local
government continues to have any local discretion
however, there will still be a case for direct
representation to it: and local voluntary
organisations are often lacking, either in the sense
of not being there, or in the sense of not being
'geared' for such representations. There is again
an argument for a new channel of communication.
    A National Social Welfare Development Council
such as has been advocated above, would no doubt in
its sector working parties go a little way to
opening up such channels. It is however not likely
to go very far in this direction, and some new
mechanism is required. Through it, it would be
possible for a local authority to augment or
complement its own services by bringing in an nvo
with resources to apply in perhaps only one or two
experimental situations: and for the latter to
identify without enormous labour where its ideas
for local initiative might be well received.
Gladstone, in the work already quoted, would
encourage this 'gradualist welfare pluralism' at
local level:

...the most attractive approach may be to weight the grant-aid allocated to local authorities and other statutory agencies. Suitable weightings could create incentives for fulfilling statutory obligations, and other commitments, through voluntary action rather than through statutory programmes. For some forms of grant-aid this would be quite simple to achieve: in the case of Urban Aid, for example, all that would be necessary would be to move away from paying 75% of the cost of projects, regardless of whether they were statutory or voluntary, towards establishing a premium for voluntary projects, which might attract say 90% of total costs while statutory programmes attract only 60%.

....in principle there is no intrinsic reason, for example, why the formula for the calculation of the Rate Support Grant (the main block of central grant-aid to local authorities averaging 61% of most local government expenditure) should not incorporate a substantial weighting in favour of local authorities which relied relatively more on voluntary welfare provision.(15)

Gladstone no doubt had local organisations only in mind. I would extend the process to national organisations.

Part of the likely future scene for nvos will increasingly be occupied by mutual aid organisations. Our study did not include them, but we have constantly been aware of them as sometimes partly integrated with, sometimes totally separate from, the 'altruistic' organisations with which we have been concerned. There is potential conflict in certain respects, - for example between the consumers pressing for immediate benefits and those who have longer term policies in mind - and certain mutual aid bodies have been described as 'hostile' to their more traditional older 'colleagues'. Only two of our sample referred to any links with mutual aid organisations in their fields. There must however be great potential advantages from organisations of both kinds working together.

A report published as this chapter was being written pinpoints some of the needs which mutual aid organisations have. The study was of local groups of four national organisations, and might be criticised for having selected better established bodies with relatively strong central supporting services: indeed three of them appeared in our own 'population' of organisations from which the sample was drawn, being considered to have wider than self-help functions.* Yet it is clear that there was widespread need for information, expert advice, voluntary helpers, 'office' services, and training for their officers. Some of these things could be provided by other voluntary organisations, either via national headquarters or by local branches encouraged and supported by their own central organisation. The report urges a 'stance' towards mutual aid groups which, whilst appreciating the limitations of their potential contribution, sees them as playing an essentially complementary role in relation to other sources of help and welcomes and supports their development. It concludes that

> Mutual aid organisations are likely to continue to thrive. There is no sign of any reduction in the enthusiasm of ordinary people for becoming involved in them. On the contrary, new organisations are still being formed and existing organisations are still sprouting new branches across the country. (16)

The wider voluntary sector of which they form a part could well resolve to take all possible steps to work with them.

At this point reference must be made to the NCVO. Those who see it as having a co-ordinating role will say that it has the job of bringing bodies in the same or contiguous or overlapping sectors together, and this will include mutual aid organisations in the process. Many others now see NCVO as having a different role: co-ordination is a fruit of co-operation, and co-operation in professional or semi-professional fields cannot well be achieved through a widely generalist body such as NCVO: specialist intermediary bodies are more suitable and capable. On the other hand there are an increasing number of activities and functions for

---

* Footnote

The four organisations were: The Royal Society for Mentally Handicapped Children & Adults (Mencap): Gingerbread: The National Association of Widows; and the National Council for the Single Woman and her Dependents (now known as The National Council for Carers and their Elderly Dependents).

which a generalist expertise, if that is not a
contradiction in terms, is called for: our sample
in the main saw the NCVO role as providing this, and
mention was made of the then topical issues of VAT
and charity law. Our study has thrown up a number
of others, such as the preparation of accounts,
methods of fund-raising, personnel management, and
knowledge and use of the parliamentary process. It
is not the function of the current study to
elaborate on or examine this important subject;
suffice it to say that this latter role for NCVO is
certainly the one to which this study points, with
the more professionally specialist functions being
left to others.

In Chapter 1 I quoted Titmuss, and in considering a likely future for voluntary organisations it
is appropriate to do so again:

> The real challenge lies in the question: what
> particular infrastructure of universalist ser-
> vices is needed in order to provide a framework
> of values and opportunity bases within and
> around which can be developed socially accept-
> able selective services aiming to discriminate
> positively, with the minimum risk of stigma, in
> favour of those whose needs are greatest.(17)

The future our study points to does not see nvos
providing the 'infrastructure of universalist
services' - that must remain with the state in the
main with a small number of exceptions. The future
for nvos lies in their pushing at the frontiers of
social provision, developing 'socially acceptable
selective services'. Even then demands or suggestions for development are going far to exceed the
possiblities of providing for them. It is essential
that nvos weigh up their own priorities very
carefully. Inevitably this will include weighing up
also the likelihood of new developments attracting
funds to support them, and this has dangers, as one
of our sample pointed out forcibly to me, of going
for the service which has sentimental appeal but may
have little else to be said for it. It also means
that if government makes known that it might support
certain kinds of development they too will have an
extra claim on the organisations' policies: this is
inevitable and, in so far as government can be
assumed not to have determined its policies lightly,
probably desirable. There will however be yet other
functions for which neither public nor government
will readily subscribe, and it is to be hoped that

nvos will continue to pursue these, in which independent trusts traditionally and rightly may be expected to be more interested.

There seems little doubt of a great future for voluntary organisations. If the prophets are right who tell us that the microchips will take care of much of the calculations and work of the future, and the economists and politicians can translate unemployment into adequate income but greater leisure for all, then there will be many more people with more opportunity for voluntary service in the widest sense of that phrase. If people continue to want to have a say in their social environment, those particularly who continue to be disillusioned with the controntation ethos of the party politics of today will find positive satisfaction in working together in voluntary organisations of the kind we have been looking at in this study. That there is much to be done in improving what such organisations are doing has been made clear, but that they are doing a worthwhile job can surely not be denied.

REFERENCES

1. Charities Aid Foundation. Charity Statistics
        1982/83.
2. Gerard, David. Charities in Britain: Conserv-
        atism or change?, (p.140). Bedford Square
        Press, London, 1983.
3. The Times, leader on 'Charitable giving and
        taking'. 17th December, 1983.
4. Ibid.
5. Waddington, David, Home Office Minister with
        responsibility for voluntary services, at
        NCVO Annual Meeting, November, 1983.
6. Quoted in Community Care, 24th November, 1983.
7. Op cit p.50.
8. Op cit p.52.
9. Government Grants. An NCVO practical guide,
        (p.2). Bedford Square Press, London, 1983.
10. Brenton, M. 'Changing Relationships in Dutch
        Social Services', in Journal of Social
        Policy, Vol. II, Part I, January 1982, (pp
        59 - 80).
11. Gladstone, F.J. Voluntary Action in a Changing
        World, (pp. 100 -101). Bedford Square
        Press, London, 1979.
12. NCVO. Beyond the Welfare State? A discussion
        paper. 1980.

13. Wilson, David C., and Butler, Richard J.
     Corporatism in the British Voluntary
     Sector. Project Working Paper
     (Unpublished).   March 1984.
14. Middlemas, Keith. 'NEDC: more than a talking
     shop', The Times, 2nd March, 1983.
15. Op cit. p.110.
16. Richardson, Ann and Goodman, Meg. Self-help
     and Social Care: Mutual Aid Organisations
     in Practice. Policy Studies Institute.,
     London, 1983.
17. Titmuss, R.M. The Gift Relationship: from
     human blood to social policy. George
     Allen and Unwin, London, 1970.

Appendix A

(Reference Chapter 2)

LIST OF ORGANISATIONS BY NAME AND DATE OF
ESTABLISHMENT WHERE KNOWN

Abbeyfield Society	1959
Age Concern England	1940
Anchor Housing Association	1968
Arthritis Care	1948
Association for Improvements in the Maternity Services	1960
Association of Jewish Refugees in Great Britain	1941
Dr Barnardo's	1866
Birth Control Campaign	1971
British Association for Early Childhood Education	1923
British Association of the Hard of Hearing	1947
British Council for Aid to Refugees	1950
British Deaf Association	1890
British Diabetic Association	1934
British Dyslexia Association	1972
British Epilepsy Association	1950
British Limbless Ex-Sevicemen's Association	1931
British Polio Fellowship	1939
British Red Cross Society	1870
British Sailors Society	1818
Brook Advisory Centres	1964
Campaign for the Advancement of State Education	not known
Camphill Village Trust Ltd	1954
Carter Foundation	1955
Catholic Housing Aid Society	1956
Catholic Marriage Advisory Council	1946
Centre for Policy on Ageing	1947
Centre on Environment for the Handicapped	1969
CHAR (Campaign for Homeless Single People)	1972
Chest, Heart and Stroke Association	1899
Christian Alliance (CAWG)	1920
Church Army	1882
Church Army Housing Limited	1924

Church of England Children's Society	1881
Church of England Council for Social Aid	1862
Colostomy Welfare Group	1967
Community Projects Foundation	1968
Contact	1965
Counsel and Care for the Elderly	1954
Crime and Justice	1979
Crossroads Care Attendant Scheme Trust	1977
Cruse (National Organisation for the Widowed and their Children)	1959
Disabled Living Foundation	1970
Distressed Gentlefolk's Aid Association	1897
Douglas Haig Memorial Homes	1929
Educational Centres Association	1920
Employment Fellowship	1921
Ex-Services Mental Welfare Society	1919
Families Need Fathers	1974
Family Planning Association	1930
Family Rights Group	1974
Family Service Units	1947
Family Welfare Association	1869
Federation of Alcoholic Residential Establishments	1974
Forces Help Society and Lord Roberts Workshops	1899
Friends of the Children Society Limited	1952
Friends of the Elderly and Gentlefolk's Help	1905
Gingerbread	1970
Guinness Trust	1890
Hanover Housing Association	1963
Housing Centre Trust	1934
Homeless Children's Aid and Adoption Society (now Mission of Hope for Children's Aid and Adoption)	1920
Howard League for Penal Reform	1866
Ileostomy Association of Great Britain & N. Ireland	1956
Independent Adoption Society	1965
Invalid Children's Aid Association	1888
Jewish Blind Society	1819
Jewish Marriage Council	1948
Jewish Welfare Board	1859
John Grooms Association for the Disabled	1866
Kings Fund Centre	1897
Lady Hoare Trust for Physically Disabled Children	1962
(The) Leonard Cheshire Foundation	1948
Marie Curie Memorial Foundation	1948
Mental After Care Association	1879
Methodist Homes for the Aged	1944
MIND (National Association for Mental Health)	1946

Motability	1977
Multiple Sclerosis Society	1953
Muscular Dystrophy Group of GB	1959
Mutual Households Association Ltd	1955
National Adoption Society	1918
NACRO (National Association for the Care and Resettlements of Offenders)	1966
National Adult School Organisation (NASO)	1899
National Association for the Welfare of Children in Hospital	1961
National Association for Maternal and Child Welfare	1911
National Association of Almshouses	1949
National Association of Citizens Advice Bureaux	1939
National Association of Leagues of Hospital Friends	1949
National Childbirth Trust	1956
National Childminding Association	1977
National Children's Bureau	1963
National Children's Home	1869
National Council for One-Parent Families	1918
National Council for the Single Woman and her Dependants	1965
National Council of Voluntary Child Care Organisations	1943
National Council on Alcoholism	1963
National Cyrenians	1970
National Deaf-Blind Helpers League	1928
National Deaf Children's Society	1944
National Elfrida Rathbone Society	1964
National Federation of Gateway Clubs	1966
National Federation of Housing Associations	1935
National Federation of Voluntary Literacy Schemes	1977
National Foster Care Association	1974
National Gypsy Education Council	1970
National Housing and Town Planning Council	1900
National Institute of Adult Education	1949
National Marriage Guidance Council	1947
National Society for Epilepsy	1892
National Society for Mentally Handicapped Children and Adults (MENCAP)	1946
National Society for the Prevention of Cruelty to Children	1884
National Women's Aid Federation	1975
Norwood, The Welfare Organisation for Jewish Children	1795
Outset	1970
Partially Sighted Society	1973
Patients Association	1963

Appendix B

(Reference Chapter 2)

OBJECTS OF THE ASSOCIATIONS IN THE SAMPLE

(Statements of objects are taken from Voluntary
Organisations. An NCVO Directory 1980/81 unless
otherwise indicated.)

British Deaf Association   BDA

The Association is concerned with the interests,
problems and needs of all deaf people, particularly
those most profoundly affected by deafness - those
who were born deaf and those who were deafened early
in life. It is an association of deaf people in
this country, and the majority of those serving on
its council are deaf. Problems of the deaf in
education, employment, and social services are
studied and information made available to interested
authorities on the experience of people suffering
the difficulties of their own lifelong deafness.
The Association represents Great Britain on the
World Federation of the Deaf and studies current
international thought and developments in health,
education and welfare. Further education presents
serious communication problems for deaf people and
the Association makes special provision for summer
schools, school-leaver courses and family summer
schools. Community holidays for elderly deaf people
are arranged where their own special needs are
catered for.

Campaign for Homeless Single People CHAR

To campaign with member organisations and homeless
people for better housing and services for people
without homes or families.

Objects of the Associations in the Sample

Chest, Heart and Stroke Association   CHSA

To work for the prevention of chest, heart and
stroke illnesses, and to help people who suffer from
them.

Church Army   CA

A Society pledged to the doctrine and practice of
the Church of England. Its officers work under the
bishops in the dioceses and the clergy in parishes
both to speed the Gospel and alleviate distress
wherever it is found.

Counsel and Care for the Elderly   CCE

To give confidential advice to anyone on all matters
of concern to elderly people or those working on
their behalf and to give financial help in cases of
need for nursing care on a temporary or permanent
basis.

Families Need Fathers   FNF

FNF is a national society primarily concerned with
the problems of maintaining a child's relationship
with both its parents during and following
separation and divorce. It gives support and help
to men and women with access and custody problems,
and seeks to change and improve the present legal
processes involved in divorce so as to eliminate
unnecessary and protracted legal conflict.

Friends of the Elderly and Gentlefolk's Help   FEGH

General financial help for the elderly and disabled
of all classes; the administration of residential
homes for gentlepeople.

Housing Centre Trust   HCT

To constitute a common meeting-ground for
organisations and individuals engaged in housing
with the object of establishing closer contact
between those working on different aspects of the
problem; to act as a clearing-house for information

and ideas on various aspects of the subject by
collecting available data relating to housing, town
and country planning, and similar subjects, and by
making this knowledge readily available; to
disseminate the information so acquired; to promote
education and research into the various branches of
the problem, and to publish memoranda.

John Grooms Association for the Disabled   JGAD

Helping the disabled to help themselves achieve the
highest possible degree of independence; providing
homes, care, work and holiday/leisure facilities.

Mission of Hope for Childrens Aid and Adoption MHCAA

The object for which the Association is formed is
the relief according to the principles and practice
of the Protestant Evangelical Faith in such manner
as the Association shall think fit of children and
young persons and their mothers and of unmarried
expectant mothers in need of care and protection.
(Memorandum of Association)

Mutual Households Association Limited   MHA

a)   To preserve for the benefit of the public
     buildings of historic or architectural interest
     or importance together with their gardens and
     grounds.
b)   To protect and augment the amenities of such
     buildings, gardens and grounds and to make
     provision for the inspection and enjoyment of
     such buildings, gardens and grounds by the
     public.
c)   For the purposes only of the principal objects
     aforesaid or any of them and as ancillary
     thereto, the Association shall have the
     following powers:

     i)   To acquire town and country houses of
          historic or architectural importance or
          interest together with the gardens and
          grounds of such houses (all such premises
          being hereafter called 'the houses').
     ii) To raise funds for the preservation of
          these houses.

iii) To convert and make alterations and additions to such parts of the houses as may not be required for public access and to let the same as residential accommodation.

iv) To provide services including meals in the houses for persons residing in or visiting the same.

v) To make regulations for the conduct of the houses including the admission of the public thereto.

(As printed in 27th Annual Report)

National Association for the Welfare of Children in Hospital NAWCH

To promote the welfare of sick children in general; to make the special needs of children in hospital more widely known; to ensure that new hospitals have adequate accommodation for mothers to live in with young children; to encourage the care of sick children at home where possible; to assist parents by providing details of visiting facilities throughout the country and to work towards the improvement of such facilities.

National Gypsy Education Council NGEC

To promote educational provision for Gypsies.

Royal Association for Disability and Rehabilitation RADAR

To improve the environment for disabled people.

The Royal British Legion Housing Association Limited RBLHA

The objects of the Society shall be to carry on the industry, business or trade of providing housing and any associated amenities for ex-Servicemen, their wives, widows and dependants, and ex-Service women, all of whom are of limited means.

(Rules of the Association)

Objects of the Associations in the Sample

Shaftesbury Homes and 'Arethusa'   Sh. H & A

To care for children in need of homes, maintenance or educational facilities and in need of financial assistance to secure such advantage.

Stonham Housing Association Ltd.   SHA

To provide throughout England and Wales, housing to help those in deprived or needful circumstances. Local voluntary groups exercise day to day management and, where required, provide social support and guidance to help the residents overcome their problems and to resume a normal place in society.

Workers' Educational Associaton   WEA

To provide adult education, independently as a responsible body recognised by the Department of Education and in co-operation with universities and local education authorities.

Appendix C

(Reference Chapter 2)

LETTER TO CHIEF EXECUTIVE OFFICERS OF SAMPLE
ORGANISATIONS

Dear Sir,
     I am writing to ask whether you and the XYZ
Association would be willing to help me in the
research which I am undertaking.
     By way of introduction, it is relevant to say
that I retired from the position of Director of the
Centre for Policy on Ageing in September 1980 after
spending most of my working life in voluntary
organisations. I am currently Chairman of the
Hanover Housing Association, an organisation
providing dwellings for the elderly throughout
England and Wales. The study I am now making is
being financed by the Joseph Rowntree Memorial
Trust.
     The object of the study is to examine the roles
of voluntary organisations in relation to the
welfare state. They may be service organisations,
pressure groups, bodies concerned mainly with study
and information, or a mixture of these. The study
presupposes that in the foreseeable future both
voluntary and statutory bodies will be concerned
with certain client needs, and that it is important
to establish what part each can reasonably play.
Considered views on this matter call for an understanding of the scale and quality of what voluntary
organisations are at present doing, and the scope
for collaboration between them and government
agencies, in promoting services in particular
fields. It will be the aim of my report to help in
this direction.
     The 'fields' referred to are those of housing,
education, health and social services. I am
concerning myself only with organisations which may
be described as 'national', not only because I
believe them to have a particular importance, but
also to make my study compassable. The method I am

186

adopting is to select a suitable sample of organisations in these fields, and to ask them to co-operate in the following ways:

1. first to provide certain factual information by post - e.g. copies of constitution and Annual Reports, and information about membership and staff;
2. then to allow me to have a longish interview (perhaps 2-3 hours) with the Chief Executive Officer, to obtain more extensive facts about the organisation and its work; followed after a week or two by
3. a similar interview with the Chairman, who would I expect wish to be accompanied by his Chief Officer, and possibly by other members of the Executive Committee. At this interview matters such as policy formation, accountability, and relationships with other voluntary bodies and with government would be discussed.

I would be grateful to know whether the XYZ Association is agreeable in principle to taking part in this project. If so I will write to you more fully about stage 1. and make tentative suggestions of dates when I might come to see you.

I shall of course be glad to answer any questions you may wish to ask before giving me your reply.

Yours faithfully,

(Signed) Hugh W. Mellor

Appendix D

(Reference Chapter 2)

INFORMATION REQUESTED BEFORE INTERVIEW

DOCUMENTS

1. A copy of the constitution/rules/memorandum and articles.

2. Copies of recent Annual Reports (the most recent and, if possible, two years previously).

3. Copies of recent statements of accounts for the same period(s).

4. Recent copies of journal(s) published by the organisation.

5. List of current publications if any.

OTHER INFORMATION IF NOT INCLUDED IN THE ABOVE

1. Date of establishment of the organisation (please give information about mergers or changes of name in the course of the organisation's history).

2. Whether organisation is registered with:
    Charity Commission
    Registrar of Friendly Societies
    Registrar of Companies
    Housing Corporation
    Other registering authority

3. Size of individual membership (if applicable).

4. Number of local branches (if any); (a list of places or other indication of their distrib-

ution throughout the country would be appreciated).

5. A list of <u>affiliated</u> <u>organisations</u> (if any) and their distribution (if not national).

6. A list of bodies to which organisation is affiliated.

7. Details of staffing, indicating roles and relevant qualifications; whether paid, unpaid or receiving honorarium: full-time or part-time; head office or branches.
   (If this detail is difficult, professional staff, with numbers of supporting staff, would be adequate.

Appendix E

(Reference Chapter 2)

INTERVIEW GUIDE – CHIEF EXECUTIVE OFFICERS

SUPPORTERS (i.e subscribers or members)

Who are the organisation's supporters?

Officials?	YES/NO
If YES, of what bodies/types of body?	
Professional people?	YES/NO
If YES, of which professions?	
Nominees of other bodies?	YES/NO
If YES, of which bodies?	
Interested members of 'the public'?	YES/NO
Other categories?	YES/NO
If YES, what are they?	

What is the number of supporters now?

Is the number increasing/remaining
steady/decreasing?

Are steps taken to 'recruit' more?   YES/NO
If YES, what steps?

Have you any indications of the loyalty/keenness of
the organisation's supporters?

e.g. what numbers attend General Meetings?
what numbers attend Conferences?
how many subscribe to your journal?

How frequently are written general reports of work
and finances prepared?

Are special reports made:

to members?   If so, in what way?
to subscribers?   If so, in what way?

to those providing grant
aid?   If so, in what way?

to others to whom organisation
has obligations?   If so, who are they?
                                   how is report
                                   made?

COMMITTEES

What are the central committees relating to policy
formation and control?

How are they constituted? (Election, nomination,
etc.)

If any members are nominated by other organisations:

    how many?
    by what organisations?
    for what reason? (constitution, condition of
    grant, etc.)

How often do they meet?

What are the skills/experience represented on
management committee(s)?

    Businessmen?   YES/NO
        If YES, detail.
    Professional people?   YES/NO
        If YES, detail.
    Political activists?   YES/NO
        If YES, are these members of
        political parties?   YES/NO
            If YES, which parties?
    Clients/Consumers per se?   YES/NO
        If YES, of what kind?
    Other?

What have been the changes in membership of
management committee(s) over the past five years?
(Information to follow if necessary)

If there are local committees, how are they
constituted?

What powers are delegated to local committees,
branches, etc?

Fund raising?	YES/NO
Appointment of staff?	YES/NO
Service to client?	YES/NO
Dealings with local authorities?	YES/NO
Other?	

Is work locally patchy, area by area?   YES/NO
    If YES, what factors account for this?
    (Wealth of area, availability of local
    residents, etc.)

INFORMATION

Is information collected systematically:

    a)   to be used in relation to service to
        clients?
    b)   to be used in formation of organisation's
        wider policies?
    c)   for consideration of government policy?

How does the organisation get its information?

    Published sources?
    Government departments?
    Other voluntary bodies?
    Committee members?
    Research instigated by organisation? (If YES,
    more later.)
    Other accumulation or collation of facts
    by staff?
        If so, is this of a kind not
        undertaken by government?   YES/NO
            If YES, please cite examples.
            Does it appear that government
            could collect it more readily?
            If NO, why does organisation
            also collect it?

Does the organisation have its own library?
(If YES, more later)

How do professional staff keep abreast of current
developments, ideas, etc?

    Journals?
        What are the main ones read?
    Conferences?
        If so, what kinds of conferences are most
        favoured?

Who organises them?
In-house arrangements?
What do they consist of?
If research is instigated by the organisation,

Is it commissioned from elsewhere?
If so, what organisations are commissioned
to do it?
Is it organised in-house?
If so, a) does organisation have a regular
budget for this purpose?
What is the amount?
b) What number of in-house projects
has organisation at present?
What sort of research does organisation
instigate?
e.g. surveys of clients/consumer views
How is it financed?
(Current examples, with grants obtained
and periods covered)

If organisation has its own library,

What is its size?
Number of items shelved?
Feet/metres of shelving?
What is its subject coverage?
What is its annual expenditure on acquisitions?
What classification system is used?
What links does it have with other libraries?
Is it used solely or largely by
organisation's own staff?   YES/NO
If NO -
Who else uses it? -
Public?
Government officials?
MPs?
Local government officials?
University research workers?
Others?
What does it have that other
libraries do not?
Is it used for reference or borrowing?
Own staff?
Others?

RELATIONSHIP WITH OTHER VOLUNTARY ORGANISATIONS

What organisations are working in the same or

overlapping fields?
(Define 'field')

Is any liaison achieved with them?
    On policy?
    On practical work?

If liaison is achieved, is it by:

    An agreement on the roles of each?
        Formal?
        Unwritten?
    Joint committees or other relationships?
    (Detail)
    Joint action on specific matters?
        Shared facilities? (Detail)
        Publishing?
        Fund-raising?
        Conference organisation?
        Representation to government?
        Other? (Detail)

What part is played in liaison by:

    NCVO?
    Local CVSs, RCCs, or equivalent bodies?
    Other intermediary bodies?

Is there any conflict with other organisations over:

    Policy? (Describe)
    Duplication of function? (Detail)
    Personal relationships?
        Central?
        Local?
    Application for statutory or other funds?
    (Detail)

RELATIONSHIP WITH STATUTORY BODIES

What central government departments does
organisation have most dealings with?
(Enlarge as appropriate on nature and frequency)

Do any statutory bodies influence organisation's
policies or practices through:

    a)   Conditions of registration? (Detail)
    b)   Conditions of grant or other funding?
          (Detail)

    c)   Conditions for agency arrangements?
        (Detail)
    d)   Monitoring exercises?

To what extent does organisation rely on government
or other statutory bodies for:

    Funds?
    Information?
    Premises?
    Staff?
    Any other support?

What other liaison is there with statutory bodies? -

    Nominations by organisation to membership of
    statutory organisations e.g. government
    advisory committees or committees of enquiry?
    (Examples)

    Personal invitations to organisation's members
    to serve on such committees?
    (Examples)

    Via national intermediary bodies? -

        NCVO?
        specialist voluntary intermediary?
        'intermediary-statutory' (e.g. AMA, ACC)?
        other?

    Other links?

Do statutory bodies use organisation for:

    Information?   YES/NO
        If YES, how is this effected?
    Policy discussions?   YES/NO
        If YES, is this through:
        Meetings with Ministers?
            How often do these occur?
        Meetings with senior civil servants?
            How often do these occur?
    Discussion of administrative matters?   YES/NO
        If YES, is this frequent/occasional/
        rare?
            If frequent, is this daily/weekly/
            monthly/less frequent?

Does organisation submit comments on Green Papers or
other consultative documents?

If so, how often does this take place?

Does organisation take steps to get government or local bodies:

a)   to take on <u>new</u> responsibilities?
b)   to increase extent of <u>current</u> responsibilities?
c)   to alter <u>ways</u> of doing things?

If so, is action mainly overt or mainly 'back-room'? (NB 'Insider' group v 'outsider' group)

<u>If</u> <u>overt</u>, does it include:
    Articles in journals?
        If so, in what journals?
        By whom?
    Own publications? (Journal/other/both)
    Own conferences?
    Own exhibition material?
    Submission of evidence to government committees and commissions of enquiry?
    Parliamentary questions?
    Circulation of material to all MPs?
    Links with parliamentary groups?
    Delegations to: MPs?
                Ministers of State?
                Government Departments at official level?
    Mass lobbies?
    Public meetings?
    Marches?
    Other demonstrations? If so, what?
    'Direct action'?   If so, what?

<u>If</u> <u>'back-room'</u>, does it include:
    Exchange of views with: Ministers?
                Civil servants at policy level?
                Political parties?
    Links with particular MPs?   YES/NO
        If YES, to provide material for speeches or questions in the House?
        To use them as advisors?
    Links with political parties?
        If so, what links?
            which parties?
    Having influential people on organisation's committees?
        MPs?

Civil servants?
Local government officers?
Local government members?
Other?
Having other people of supposed influence playing other parts in the organisation? (e.g. peers, public figures in special fields)

Does organisation seek to have titled people as Patron, President, etc?

Has organisation any <u>measure</u> of its <u>impact</u> on:

a) Public opinion? (e.g. numbers of articles in different journals, numbers of mentions in media, publications sold)
b) Parliament? (e.g. numbers of parliamentary questions)
c) Civil servants?

What part is played by <u>local</u> organisations or branches in exerting influence on <u>national</u> policy?

Has organisation any evidence of <u>effects</u> of its activities on:

a) Legislation?   If so, what are recent examples?
b) Delegated legislation?   If so, what are recent examples?
c) Departmental practices?   If so, what are recent examples?

Has organisation introduced pioneer schemes aimed at influencing national policy by example?

If so, is there in-built monitoring/evaluation of such schemes?
If so, of what does this consist?
Are they written up to maximise knowledge of their experience or findings?

POLICY FORMATION

Does <u>broad</u> policy stem from the views of:

    organisation's own members?
    organisation's own subscribers?
    clients/consumers?
    staff?
    central government?
    local government?
    other sources?   (If so, define)

Has <u>formal machinery</u> been established to ensure that the <u>views of any of</u> the above are made known?

Would you say that policies resulting measure up to needs and opportunities? (Pointer to other sources of policy formation)

To what extent are major decisions influenced by:

    what will attract financial support from:
        subscribers?   Major/minor/no influence
        trusts?   Major/minor/no influence
        fees?   Major/minor/no influence

    response to specific pressure
    from government, local
    government, or other statutory
    sources?   Major/minor/no influence

        if this is an influence, is it more likely
        to be positive (i.e. encouragement in
        certain directions) or negative
        (inhibition of certain work or
        activities)?

response to broad policy
statements by
government?   Major/minor/no influence

desire to continue long-
standing services/traditions/
loyalty to founder
etc?   Major/minor/no influence

desire to pioneer?   Major/minor/no influence

response to new research
or information?   Major/minor/no influence

leads from CEO or
other staff?   Major/minor/no influence

Is there conflict at times between any of the above?
(e.g. response to research conclusions v problems of
raising funds, pioneering v extending existing
work)

Do the terms of trust, or the constitution, of the
organisation prove restrictive on what it would like
to undertake?

Are the terms closely adhered to?

THE EXECUTIVE/MANAGEMENT COMMITTEE

(CEO has given me the skills/experience available on
the committee)

Has committee all the weight and experience it needs
at present?

If not, in what ways is it lacking?
    Certain expertise or experience?
    (NB Is it 'one-class'?)
    Intelligent interest?
    People with time to give for subcommittee
    work etc?
    Other?

How far is committee membership representative of
the sectors listed above? -

members?
subscribers?
clients/consumers?

other bodies in the field?
staff?
central government?
local government?

Does committee think that it could/should be representative of these sectors?

If statutory bodies nominate members of organisation's committee(s):

what sort of person is nominated?
   are their qualifications relevant?
   is their interest manifest?
are they valuable as links?
are they valuable as members otherwise?

Is committee membership reviewed regularly?

If so: how?
      how often?
      how are possible new members discovered?
      what criteria are used in selection of
      new names? (expertise, time, eminence,
      etc.)

Is there difficulty in getting suitable new members of committee?

If so: why?
      time involved in the work?
      expense?
      other?

What do you think attracts people to support the organisation?

Does the organisation consider that it is adequately meeting modern demands for accountability?

Please cite ways considered important (Annual Reports, Annual Meetings, representation of funding bodies on the committee etc.)

Proposals have been made in various quarters -

a)   that voluntary organisations should be
      required to conduct their affairs
      according to regulations laid down by law
      and/or
b)   that those which receive say 50% or more

of their income from public funds should
be made directly accountable to
Parliament.

What are your views on these suggestions?

RELATIONSHIP WITH OTHER VOLUNTARY ORGANISATIONS

What are the attitudes of committee members to other
voluntary organisations in the field?
(Tolerance/hostility/competitiveness/eagerness
to work with them)

Is there public criticism of there being several
organisations in the field?

What is the response of committee members
individually and collectively to charges:

of wasteful duplication?
of lack of co-operation?
of lack of cross-fertilisation of ideas?

Do statutory bodies understand differences of role?

If there are bilateral agreements to co-operate with
any other organisations, how effective are they?
(Detail)

If intermediary bodies take steps to effect co-
operation, does committee consider them to be
effective?

Is it inevitable that statutory bodies 'hold the
ring' between voluntary organisations:

competing for grant aid?
wishing to undertake agency functions?
which are brought into consultation processes?
expressing views on government policy changes
required?

If not, what alternatives are there?

e.g. establishment of spokesmen for sectors of
the field, as AMA/ACC for local authority
Personal Social Services, or Independent
Development Council for Mentally Handicapped
People.

INFLUENCING NATIONAL POLICY AND PRACTICE

(Reference back to membership of organisation and committee)

To what extent is influence dependent upon a valid claim to represent a distinct and cohesive section of society?

> Can the organisation substantiate such a claim?

How much weight is given to influence exerted in the various ways already discussed with the CEO? (Go through item by item).

(If not covered by discussion on Accountability) Does the organisation feel inhibited by its charitable status from action aimed at influencing national policy?

Is there a need for a body to provide a united voice to government on issues wider than the organisation's own? (e.g. local government social services, hospital care)

> How far do existing bodies meet this need? (Identify bodies)

Can there be a conflict between the organisation doing something that needs to be done, and influencing government to do it, i.e. can doing it have a negative effect on getting a national policy? (If so, illustrate with examples).

PHILOSOPHY OF WELFARE STATE

Does organisation see the service with which its work is concerned as:

> a)   Ideally to be provided solely by non-statutory bodies (voluntary or private)?
>   If so, can they provide a consistent (non-patchy) service?
> b)   Ideally to be provided solely by the State?
> c)   Ideally to be provided by statutory and non-statutory?
>   If so, would services of each be: supplementary (same)?

complementary (different in some
way)?
Is there a risk of one source
(statutory or non-statutory) being
regarded as inferior in status?

In sum, how does the organisation see the role of
the voluntary organisation <u>vis-a-vis</u> the state:

a)   ideally?
b)   in long-term practice?

Appendix F

(Reference Chapter 3)

COMPARATIVE EXPENDITURE ON ADMINISTRATION

One aspect of an examination of any organisation which always, and rightly, excites attention, is whether it is employing staff in the most economical way, yet without unduly impairing efectiveness and efficiency. This is especially the case where charitable organisations are concerned, for there is the responsibility to make good use of money subscribed for specific purposes: the confidence and trust of donors must be maintained, but there is also the additional responsibility, of which most trustees will be very conscious, to treat staff fairly. This means not only paying fair salaries, but also employing a number and kind of staff commensurate with the work to be done: too few staff sharing too much work is probably a common condition of many voluntary bodies and to some extent this is creditable, but it can also lead to inefficiency or breakdown, whether personal or organisational. Yet it is desirable, if it can be achieved, also to have answers to critics who suspect that welfare organisations have too many staff, i.e. that there is under-employment in their ranks.

To achieve any objective measures of these matters which are fully satisfactory to all is almost certainly impossible. Accountants and their clients are unable it seems even to agree forms of accounts which describe the condition of the organisation in ways which are apt, as well as being correct. A first thought on this might be one of surprise where staffing is concerned: it is surely perfectly easy to include a figure for salaries paid. No doubt that is so, but in fact very few statements of accounts do this, for the possibly good reason that such a figure would be misunderstood. As implied above, whether or not such a figure is reasonable depends very much on the

kind of organisation and the work to be done. In
the past there has been a tendency to take such a
figure and relate it to total expenditure, with a
criticism implied if the resultant percentage was in
double figures: or to divide it by the number of
staff and draw conclusions from the average salary.
Such exercises may be totally misleading and
charitable organisations take steps to make it
impossible to undertake them. (Only four
organisations in the sample of 16 of those which
employed staff showed figures which facilitated
these kinds of analysis. Average salaries varied
between £3,500 and £8,642. Salaries expenditure
between 46% and 70% of total expenditure).

In this study all the organisations had one
thing in common - that their staff were serving a
country-wide movement from a central headquarters.
The services they provided were different, in ways
which the study has pin-pointed, yet all were
basically a modest sized office administration with
a number of specialist officers on the staff. It
seemed reasonable to think there should be some way
to make comparison between them, after making due
allowance for obvious differences. As has been
stated there were few figures for expenditure on
salaries, and it seemed unreasonable, if not
impracticable, to ask for them. There were however
total administrative costs, and the numbers of staff
were known. Would a figure of expenditure per head
of staff be significant?

Looking at each of the sixteen organisations
with this in mind first reflections on what might be
undertaken and what results expected were:

BDA	produce a number of publications which might put their 'index no.' of expenditure divided by number of staff above average.
CHAR	publications may lift above the average
CHSA	likewise have extensive publications and probably expensive offices, so would be on the high side. Their expenditure on grants would of course not be included.
CA	probably average.
CCE	are totally casework oriented, i.e. staff-intensive, which would make their index no. low. Their expenditure on welfare grants to individuals would be excluded.
FEGH	apparently a purely administrative function, so would be near or possibly a little lower than average.

Comparative Expenditure on Administration

HCT	administration largely, so probably average.
JGAD	probably average.
MHCAA	probably average.
MHA	possibly above average as offices are probably expensive.
NAWCH	mainly administrative, probably average.
RADAR	the largest bar RBLHA with a variety of activity, so probably should be near average.
RBLHA	the largest, but also includes regional staff and offices in the calculation so probably low.
Sh. H & A	similar organisation to JGAD, similar index no. might be expected.
SHA	similar set-up to RBLHA, probably therefore also near average.
WEA	mainly administrative, near average.

The actual 'index numbers' in £000 produced by this process were as follows:

Organisation	Expenditure on central admin. £000s	Number of staff	Expenditure per head. £000s
BDA	499	30	16.63
CHAR	73.6	6	12.27
CHSA	397	26	15.27
CA	466	70	6.67
CCE	80	13	6.15
FEGH	203	20	10.15
HCT	50.4	4	12.61
JGAD	207	22	9.41
MHCAA	63.5	7	9.07
MHA	143	8.5	16.82
NAWCH	62.5	7	8.93
RADAR	515	50	10.30
RBLHA*	939.6	105	8.95
SH. H & A	118	8	14.75
SHA	180.8	14	12.91
WEA	89.4	8	11.17

* Footnote

Includes regional offices

206

Comparative Expenditure on Administration

The median figure is 10.74, from which it will be
seen that of the expected results:

BDA is above average, as expected.
CHAR is slightly above average.
CHSA is on the high side as expected.
CA is well below the average expected.
CCE is much the lowest, as expected.
FEGH is just below average, as expected.
HCT is above the average expected.
JGAD is slightly less than the average expected
MHCAA is less than the average expected.
MHA is above the average as expected.
NAWCH is slightly less than the average expected
RADAR is near average, as expected.
RBLHA is lower than the average, as expected.
Sh. H & A is surprisingly higher than expected.
SHA is higher than the average expected.
WEA is very near the average, as expected.

There is a pleasing degree of 'fit' between
what was expected and what was found, which gives
confidence in the process, and reason to think that
the exceptions to the fit are worth further
comments. These are CA, JGAD, MHCAA and NAWCH whose
index numbers are lower than expected, and HCT and
Sh. H & A which are higher. From lower figures one
might conclude that the work is labour intensive
undertaken with relatively little use of resources
in equipment, or travelling, or office
accommodation: or that expenditure is kept low, on
overheads by having less expensive offices (CA,
JGAD, MHCAA and NAWCH might all fall into that
category), or by paying staff less than others do.
From higher figures the reverse could be concluded -
if for example there were a larger than average
number of higher paid specialist staff, or costly
central offices, or extensive travelling: none of
these on the face of it apply to the two
organisations concerned, though one feature common
to them is that the number of staff is very small, 4
and 8 respectively, which could make higher index
numbers almost inevitable; though MHCAA with 7 staff
and NAWCH with 8 have kept their figures low.
This little exercise is relegated to an
appendix because it is recognised that its standing
is not great. The writer believes that the index
has some validity if carefully used, and may be of
interest to some readers.

Appendix G

(Reference Chapter 5)

ORGANISATIONS WORKING IN THE SAME OR OVERLAPPING
FIELDS

BDA   British Association of the Hard of Hearing
         National Deaf Children's Society
         Royal National Institute for the Deaf
CHAR   Church Army
         Shelter
         National Association for the Care and
              Resettlement of Offenders (NACRO)
         MIND
         Federation of Alcoholic Residential
              Establishments (FARE)
         Child Poverty Action Group
CHSA   Action on Smoking and Health (ASH)
         Asthma Research Council
         British Heart Foundation
CA   Age Concern England
         CHAR
         Family Welfare Association
         Josephine Butler Association
         National Association of Voluntary Hostels
         National Council for Voluntary Youth
              Service
CCE   Age Concern England
         Disabled Living Foundation
FNF   Campaign for Justice in Divorce
         National Council for One-Parent Families
         Gingerbread
         National Marriage Guidance Council
         Family Rights Group
         Family Action Group of the Order of
              Christian Unity
FEGH   Distressed Gentlefolks Association
         Age Concern England
         Royal United Kingdom Beneficent
              Association
HCT   National Federation of Housing
              Associations

	Institute of Housing
	Shelter
JGAD	Shaftesbury Society
	RADAR
	Disabled Living Foundation
	Holiday Care Association
MHCAA	British Association of Adoption and Fostering Agencies
	National Council for One-Parent Families
	National Children's Bureau
MHA	Historic Houses Association
	Headbourne Worthy
NAWCH	National Children's Bureau
NGEC	Advisory Council for the Education of Romanies and other Travellers (ACERT)
	National Gypsy Council
	Romany Guild
	Association of Gypsy Organisations
RADAR	Disabled Living Foundation
	Spastics Society
	Multiple Sclerosis Society of Great Britain and Northern Ireland
	Muscular Dystrophy Group of Great Britain
	Disability Alliance
	Child Poverty Action Group
RBLHA	Anchor Housing Association
	Hanover Housing Association
Sh. H & A	Church of England Children's Society
	Dr. Barnardo's
	National Children's Home
SHA	National Association for the Care and Resettlement of Offenders (NACRO)
	MIND
	National Council on Alcoholism
WEA	National Institute of Adult Education

Appendix H

(Reference Chapter 5)

BODIES TO WHICH ORGANISATIONS IN THE SAMPLE ARE AFFILIATED

BDA	NCVO
CHAR	Child Poverty Action Group
	Howard League for Penal Reform
	MIND (National Association for Mental Health)
	National Association for the Care and Resettlement of Offenders
	National Cyrenians
	Radical Alternatives to Prison
	Shelter
CHSA	None
CA	CHAR
	Council of Voluntary Welfare Work
	NCVO
	Partners in World Mission (and other Anglican bodies)
CCE	Age Concern England
FNF	Family Forum
HCT	NCVO
FEGH	None
JGAD	Disability Rights Association
	Holiday Care Association
	NCVO
	RADAR
MHCAA	British Associaton of Adoption and Fostering Agencies
	National Council of Voluntary Child Care Organisations
MHA	None
NAWCH	Exodus
	Fair Play for Children
	Family Forum
	Independent Council for Mentally Handicapped
	Maternity Alliance
	National Children's Bureau

Bodies to which Organisations are Affiliated

NAWCH (cont)	NCVO National Council of Women Play in Hospital Liaison Committee Standing Conference of Women's Organisations Voluntary Organisations Liaison Council for the Under-Fives
NGEC	None
RADAR	NCVO
RBLHA	National Federation of Housing Associations
Sh.H & A	National Council of Voluntary Child Care Organisations
SHA	Housing Centre Trust Industrial Society National Association for the Care and Resettlement of Offenders National Association of Voluntary Hostels NCVO National Federation of Housing Associations
WEA	NCVO National Institute of Adult Education

Appendix J

(Reference Chapter 7)

FUND RAISING APPEALS

The author's household may be as typical as any in
its experience of appeals from charities through the
post. If it is, there is real cause for concern at
the methods some charities are using. I quote three
recent examples.

<u>Charity</u> <u>A.</u>   (Cancer)

     Letters of appeal received November 1980, July
1981, December 1981, May 1982. When taxed with the
frequency with which they were being received, the
CEO wrote in August 1982:

     I am greatly obliged for your letter of 13th
     August and for drawing to my personal attention
     the duplication of our appeals. I am also
     concerned to learn that you failed to receive a
     reply to your letter of July last year since we
     do endeavour to be punctilious in answering
     correspondence. My apologies for this apparent
     but unintentional discourtesy.
          Since our appeal material has to be
     prepared well in advance of despatch, I fear
     you will undoubtedly receive this year's
     Christmas Appeal. To avoid in future the mid-
     year duplication I shall be grateful if you
     will either ignore the Christmas Appeal, or,
     should you still feel kindly disposed towards
     (Charity A), perhaps you will, when responding,
     mark your remittance form boldly to the effect
     "NO MID YEAR APPEAL TO BE SENT".

Despite this moderately worded explanation, the
situation cannot be said to be satisfactory, and it
is maintained by a number of other charities that -
despite this computerised age, or because of it -

212

they cannot stop repetitive appeals reaching even those who have already subscribed. This is an abuse of the disorganised and the soft-hearted, many of whom are elderly and less well-to-do: it is an irritant to those who <u>are</u> well organised, even if it does not drive them away; and on the face of it, it is a waste of money, though no doubt appeals organisers would argue with this. Whatever else, it tarnishes the general image of charitable organisations.

<u>Charity</u> <u>B</u>.   (Children)

Dear Mr X,

We are enclosing with this letter what we regard as an extremely valuable map of the world. Please take just a few minutes to unfold and examine it, since it is a special and very unusual map. It shows the world as it really is. With new dimensions. With better proportions. In fact, a completely different picture of our planet. In Aylesbury, nobody dies of hunger. Yet less than 8 hours flying time from the UK children die every day from malnutrition and related diseases. Not only in Ethiopia. Not only in Bangladesh. But in over 100 countries where Y is working. <u>40,000</u> children die every day. Thousands <u>more lose</u> their sight - from a simple lack of vitamins. Y is looking for people who understand the responsibility we all have towards the world's children. Y needs an informed public - a public which understands the realities of life in this world we all share. We need <u>your</u> support and <u>your</u> care for the children of the world.
If you, Mr X, wish to support Y's vast and pressing task please use the payment slip below and post it to us today. And with this map please accept our thanks.
Yours sincerely,

AB
<u>Director</u>

P.S. If you do not wish to keep this special map, please return it to us. In this way you can help us to save costs. Thank you very much.

Again this is illustrative of other examples, in which the personalised but unknown recipient is sent something "extremely valuable" with the request either to subscribe; or return (in this case) the map without a subscription (which would cost postage and make the sender feel mean); or to keep the map and send nothing (which would - unless one felt very belligerent, as the present recipient did, make one feel even meaner). This is an elementary form of blackmail.

Charity C.   (Deaf)

This letter was sent to a lady aged 94 and stone-deaf. It was, of course, not to be expected that the charity knew this, but it adds point to the criticism of it.

Dear Mrs. X,

We need your support again Mrs X.
For several years now Mrs. X I have looked upon you as one of Z's friends and supporters. You have in the past generously supported Z and have helped our work for the 10 million deaf people in Britain. But, for reasons I'm not aware of you've suddenly stopped supporting us Mrs. X.
I have appealed to you for help on a number of occasions over the past couple of years, but I haven't heard from you. Have you moved home or have your circumstances changed? Mrs. X, I really can't believe that you don't want to support Z any more. You know that through your support Mrs. X we've been able to create some wonderful and essential facilities for deaf people. Places like A which has a unit for young people who are deaf and blind. Or B for deaf young people who've also had major emotional problems.
Put yourself in the shoes of those young people Mrs. X. Would you want to think that someone had suddenly lost interest in you?
In the year ahead, we have an urgent need to raise money to help pay for a number of important projects.
(Here follow several examples)
But all these things cost money Mrs. X.
That's why your help and support is so important to us. We needed you in the 70's, we

need you just as much in 1983.

In fact, there are 10 million deaf people who
need your help Mrs. X. This year, next year
and in the future.
Because you've given to Z before will you
do so again now? Whatever you give it will
help because every little extra adds up. And
it means we will be able to provide the
services deaf people urgently need. They look
to Z for help. And Z looks to you Mrs. X.
With this letter is a simple coupon to use
when you make your donation. We've printed
your address on it but if you have moved do
please let us know.
Mrs. X, I hope we can count on your
support this Christmas.
Yours sincerely,

The hectoring tone of this letter is thoroughly
shameful, and makes no allowance for all sorts of
possible good reasons why support earlier given
might no longer be continued. It would certainly
cause many timid and forgetful but well-intentioned
old ladies to send money they could ill afford. It
is made very much worse by being in this case
totally untrue, in that

a) she had not been a supporter before
b) she had not had "a number of" appeals over
the past two years.